Praise for *Arizona 1*

"Here is a real fundamental basic crash course in Arizona law. Everything is taken care of in this book...You can find out more than you ever dreamed."

　　　　—Pat McMahon, *The Pat McMahon Show*,
　　　　KAZTV, Phoenix

"I love this book...it's a marvelous undertaking...simple to use; easy to understand...this book is so relevant...a tremendous amount of information."

　　　　—John C. Scott, radio talk show host,
　　　　KJLL, 1330 AM, Tucson

"Interpreting the legal jargon and navigating the various laws can be a daunting task for even a trained professional. That's why *Arizona Laws 101: A Handbook for Non-Lawyers* is so helpful. Written specifically for the layperson, 101 Arizona laws are interpreted and spelled out in a way that easily lays out the principles."

　　　　—*BizAZ Magazine*

"Cutting through the Latin phrases and complex case law recitations that confuse laypeople, the softcover book explains the basics of our state's laws...[*Arizona Laws 101*] will allow you to be much better informed, and it's the sort of reference volume from which anyone can benefit."

　　　　—*Tucson Lifestyle Magazine*

"[A] great service and resource for the citizens of Arizona."

　　　　—Hon. Christopher Skelly, Maricopa County
　　　　superior court judge (ret.)

"What an invaluable reference. You have done a real service for both non-lawyers and lawyers."

　　　　—Merton E. Marks, Esq., arbitrator and
　　　　mediator

"It is important to have this book if you moved here from somewhere else…it gives you guidelines, a place to go."
—*AM Arizona*, KAZ-TV, Prescott

"This is a great reference point for people learning on the fly."
—*Good Morning Tucson*, KGUN, Tucson

"This book may answer a lot of your questions…good information."
—*Arizona Midday*, KPNX, Phoenix

"A tool that will help answer the most common legal questions you may have."
—*Arizona Morning*, KSAZ Fox, Phoenix

"You did good work on this…it's got everything in it."
—*Good Morning Arizona*, KTVK, Phoenix

"This makes it really easy [to read]…it's not that legalese that we hear sometimes."
—*News 4 at 4*, KVOA, Tucson

Arizona Laws 101

Arizona Laws 101

a handbook for non-lawyers

2nd Edition

Donald A. Loose

Arizona Laws 101: A Handbook for Non-Lawyers

Published by Fenestra Books®
1760 East River Road, Suite 145
Tucson, Arizona 85718 USA
www.fenestrabooks.com

Publisher's Cataloging-in-Publication
(Provided by Quality Books, Inc.)

Loose, Donald A.
Arizona laws 101: a handbook for non-lawyers /
[Donald A. Loose].
p. cm.
LCCN 2005928725
ISBN 1-58736-522-7

1. Law--Arizona--Popular works. I. Title.
II. Title: Arizona laws one hundred one III. Title: Arizona
laws one hundred and one

KFA2481.L66 2005 349.791
QBI05-600088

For Nancy

Contents

Part Three: Family Law

Part Four: Wills and Estates

Part Five: Civil Lawsuits and Claims

Part Six: Business Law

Appendices

Author's Note &
Acknowledgements

The first edition of this book was published in 2005. Since that time, in Arizona several controversial immigration bills have been passed and signed into law—only to be challenged in the courts; a well-known and once popular Arizona state senator was recalled from office presumably over his sponsorship of controversial legislation; and hundreds of Arizona laws, many of which are included in this book, have been changed by subsequent legislation or court decisions. Indeed, the legal landscape in Arizona changes quickly, and it was time for a second edition.

In writing the second edition, I did several things: I updated each chapter to include all changes to the law since the first edition; at the request of readers, I added three new chapters—gun laws, homeowner associations, and non-profit corporations; and I combined three previous chapters with three other existing chapters, to keep the total number of chapters at 101. This second edition is thus completely new and revised, but in many ways it remains the same as the first.

I am proud to say that this book won a 2007 Glyph Award from the Arizona Book Publishers Association, in the education/teaching/academic category. It also has received critical acclaim from the Arizona press, broadcast media, and my fellow attorneys. But I'm most proud of the fact that Arizona

Laws 101 is now in more than 100 libraries in the state of Arizona, and is being used by library patrons throughout the state to educate themselves about Arizona laws.

Arizona Laws 101 is, first and foremost, a handbook for non-lawyers. I attempted to write each chapter in such a way that a person without legal training will have no difficulty understanding the legal principles discussed. It is my hope that a person in need of legal information will find in this book a succinct summary of the law in which he or she is interested, and then, if an attorney is needed, be a better consumer of legal services by reason thereof.

In this book, I frequently use *he, his* and *him*, instead of *she, hers* or *her*. No discrimination is intended. Under the rules of English grammar, the pronouns he, his and him may generally be used to stand for the common gender. The pronouns she, hers and her, by contrast, refer only to the feminine gender. To avoid using a feminine gender pronoun where no specific gender was intended, I chose instead to use a common gender pronoun. The reader is thus free to assume whatever gender he or she desires.

I owe a debt of gratitude to Joshua Furman, Leighten Hendrickson, Kyle Brown, Rob Hobkirk, Jesse Callahan, and Mark Jacobson for their invaluable assistance in producing a second edition. Josh and Mark, law clerks both, researched the laws and noted important changes since the first edition; my legal partners, Kyle, Rob, and Jesse, read various chapters and provided me their knowledgeable insights and comments; and Leighten, my editorial assistant (and herself law school-bound), read the entire draft, twice, and suggested a myriad of grammatical and punctuation changes. The book is indisputably better because of their efforts.

I would like to thank John C. Scott and Bill Buckmaster, two of the best broadcasters in Arizona, for their generous support and many kind comments about this book. In the years since this book was first published, I have appeared regularly on both of their radio shows to discuss current legal topics and events. I have enjoyed my long-time association with each of them, and I look forward to the interviews to come in the years ahead. Better friends an author could not have.

Lastly, I would like to thank my wife, Nancy, for her continual enthusiasm, support, and patience for this project. Without her, this book would not exist.

Don Loose
March 2012

Introduction

This is a handbook for non-lawyers. It has been written so that a person without legal training should be able to readily understand the principles set forth. The 101 laws covered in this book have been selected because of their relevance to events occurring in everyday life.

While this book does contain legal information, it is not a substitute for qualified legal advice. The reader is advised to seek legal counsel regarding any legal matter discussed in this book. The author does not purport to give legal advice to the reader.

Because this is a handbook of Arizona laws, federal laws have not been included. Accordingly, the reader will not find any detailed information about bankruptcy, federal trademark registration, or any other subject governed by federal law. This book does, however, include the laws that every Arizona resident needs to know to be a responsible citizen of the 48th state!

Arizona Laws 101

PART ONE

Criminal & Traffic Laws; Citizens' Rights and Duties

1

Driving Under the Influence (DUI)

"[A] terrible toll [is] taken, both in personal injuries and property damage, by drivers who mix alcohol and gasoline." —The Arizona Supreme Court

It is illegal to drive or to be in physical control of a vehicle in Arizona 1) while under the influence of alcohol or any drug, or 2) within two hours of having an alcohol concentration of .08 or more, or 3) while there is any illegal drug or metabolite (metabolism-produced substance) in the body. Violation of Arizona's DUI law will subject the offender to jail time, loss of license, and monetary fines and assessments. In extreme cases, the drunk driver may be sent to prison and have his car taken from him.

If proven in a trial that there was .05 or less alcohol concentration in the person's blood or breath within two hours of the time of driving, it will be presumed that he was *not* under the influence of alcohol; if there was in excess of .05 but less than .08 alcohol concentration, no presumption will arise either way; and, if there was .08 or more alcohol concentration, it will be presumed that the person was under the influence of alcohol. Remember, however, that whether or not a person is found to have been "under the influence" of alcohol, it is still illegal to drive within two hours of having an alcohol concentration of .08 or more. Please refer to Appendix A for charts showing approximate blood alcohol percentages for men and women, based on number of drinks and body weight.

A person who is convicted of DUI will be sentenced to serve not less than 10 days in jail; pay fines and assessments of not less than $1,250; be required to complete alcohol or other drug screening; and be required to equip his vehicle with an ignition interlock device. In addition, the person may be required to perform community restitution. The judge may suspend all but one day of the jail sentence if the person completes a court-ordered alcohol or other drug screening, education or treatment program.

If the results of a person's blood or alcohol breath test show .08 or more alcohol concentration, the Department of Transportation will suspend that person's driver license for 90 days. If the person is employed or attending school, then the Department will suspend the person's license for 30 days, and restrict his driving privileges for an additional 60 days to travel between home and work, or between home and school. This reduced suspension is available only if the person did not cause a death or serious physical injury, there are no prior DUI convictions or driver license suspensions within the past 84 months, and the person completes mandated alcohol or other drug screening.

Second-Time Offenders

If a person is convicted of a second DUI offense within 84 months (seven years), he will be sentenced to serve not less than 90 days in jail, 30 days of which must be served consecutively; be ordered to pay fines and assessments of not less than $3,000; have his driver license revoked for one year; be required to equip his vehicle with an ignition interlock device; and be ordered to perform at least 30 hours of community restitution. The judge may suspend all but 30 days of the jail sentence if the person completes an alcohol or other drug screening, education or treatment program.

Extreme DUI

A person who has an alcohol concentration of .15 or more within two hours of driving or being in actual physical control

4

of a vehicle is guilty of extreme DUI. A person convicted of this offense will be sentenced according to his alcohol concentration, as explained below.

If the alcohol concentration was .15 or more but less than .20, the person will be sentenced to serve not less than 30 consecutive days in jail; be ordered to pay fines and assessments of not less than $2,500; have his driver license suspended for 90 days (subject to the same restricted driving privileges discussed above); and be required to equip his vehicle with an ignition interlock device. In addition, the person may be ordered to perform community restitution. The judge may suspend all but nine days of the sentence if the person equips his vehicle with an ignition interlock device for 12 months.

If the alcohol concentration was .20 or more, the same penalties as above apply, except the person will be sentenced to serve not less than 45 consecutive days in jail, and to pay fines and assessments of not less than $2,750. The judge may suspend all but 14 days of the sentence if the person equips his vehicle with an ignition interlock device for 12 months.

If a person is convicted of a second extreme DUI within 84 months and his alcohol concentration was less than .20, he will be sentenced to serve not less than 120 days in jail, 60 of which must be served consecutively; be ordered to pay fines and assessments of not less than $3,250; have his driver license revoked for one year; be required to equip his vehicle with an ignition interlock device; and be ordered to perform at least 30 hours of community restitution.

If a person is convicted of a second extreme DUI within 84 months and his alcohol concentration was .20 or more, he will be sentenced to serve not less than 180 days in jail, 90 of which must be served consecutively; be ordered to pay fines and assessments of not less than $3,750; have his driver license revoked for one year; be required to equip his vehicle with an ignition interlock device; and be ordered to perform at least 30 hours of community restitution.

Aggravated DUI

A person is guilty of aggravated driving while under the influence if he does any of following:

- Drives or controls a vehicle while under the influence of alcohol or drugs while his driver license is suspended, canceled, revoked, refused or restricted as a result of a prior DUI.
- Commits a third or subsequent violation of the DUI laws within a period of 84 months.
- Drives or controls a vehicle while under the influence of alcohol or drugs while a person under 15 years of age is in the vehicle.
- While he is required to equip his vehicle with an ignition interlock device, drives or controls a vehicle while under the influence of alcohol or drugs.

If a person is convicted of aggravated DUI under section 1 above or for a third DUI within 84 months under section 2, he will be sentenced to serve not less than four months in *prison*. If a person is convicted of a fourth or subsequent DUI under section 2 above, he will be sentenced to serve not less than eight months in *prison*. If a person is convicted of aggravated DUI under section 3 above, he will be sentenced to at least the minimum sentence imposed for the DUI offense he commits.

The Department of Transportation will revoke the person's driver license for one year, and the court may order an interlock device on the person's vehicle for more than 24 months after his driving privileges are reinstated. The person will also be assessed fines and penalties of not less than $4,000, and he will be ordered to attend and complete alcohol or other drug screening, education or treatment from an approved facility. In addition, the vehicle owned and operated by a person convicted of aggravated DUI will be forfeited and disposed of according to law.

Aggravated DUI is a felony.

Other DUI Facts:

- A person convicted of DUI must usually pay the costs of court-ordered screening, education or treatment.
- The fines and assessments imposed in DUI cases are generally subject to substantial surcharges, which must be paid in addition to the fines and assessments.
- A person who is sentenced to serve time in jail or prison must reimburse the government for the costs of his incarceration, in an amount determined by the court.
- A person has a right to trial by jury if charged with a repeat offense, extreme DUI, or aggravated DUI, but not simple drunken driving.
- More stringent standards are imposed on commercial drivers (an alcohol concentration of .04 is the legal limit).

2

Implied Consent
(Blood and Breath Alcohol Tests)

"Driving is a privilege, not a right." —U.S. Supreme Court

Every person who operates a motor vehicle in Arizona automatically gives consent to a test or tests of his blood, breath, urine or other bodily substance. The test or tests may be administered by a law enforcement officer after a person is arrested for driving under the influence of intoxicating liquor or drugs or, if the person is under 21 years of age, for driving with liquor in his body. A law enforcement officer who has reasonable suspicion to believe that a person is driving under the influence may request that the person submit to a preliminary breath test or tests before an arrest.

After an arrest, the person will be requested to submit to one or more tests for the purpose of determining alcohol concentration or drug content. If the person refuses, he will be informed that his driver license will be suspended for 12 months, or for two years for a second refusal within a period of 84 months, unless he agrees to submit to and successfully complete the test or tests. A failure to expressly agree to the test or to successfully complete the test is deemed a refusal. He will also be informed that: 1) if the test results show a blood or breath alcohol concentration of .08 or more, his driver license will be suspended for not less than 90 days; and 2) his driving privilege may be reinstated following the suspension only if he completes alcohol or other drug screening.

A person who is dead, unconscious, or otherwise in a condition rendering him incapable of refusal is deemed to give consent to any test or tests that may be performed by law enforcement.

If a person refuses to submit to a test requested by law enforcement, the test will not be given. In that case, the officer will require the immediate surrender of the person's driver license, issue an order of suspension, and issue a temporary driving permit that will remain valid for 15 days. The officer will also notify the Department of Transportation of the refusal.

The driver has the right to request a hearing before the Department of Transportation to contest the suspension. The hearing generally must be requested within 15 days after the issuance of the order of suspension. If a request for hearing is not timely made, or if the Department determines to uphold the suspension order after a hearing, the person's driver license will be suspended for 12 months, or for a period of two years if the suspension was for a second or subsequent refusal within a period of 84 months.

A person who is unsuccessful at a suspension hearing may ask the superior court to review the Department's decision. However, a driver's chances of success here are not good, in that the vast majority of suspension orders are upheld by the court.

After completing not less than 90 days of the suspension period and any alcohol or other drug screening that is ordered by the Department, a person whose driving privilege is suspended may apply to the Department for a special ignition interlock restricted driver license. A person who is issued such a restricted license must maintain a functioning certified ignition interlock device during the remaining period of the suspension. A special ignition interlock restricted driver license is not, however, available to a person whose driving privilege is suspended for a second or subsequent refusal within a period of 84 months, or a person who within a period of 84 months has been convicted of a second or subsequent violation of 1) driving under the influence, or 2) if under the age of 21 years, driving or being in physical control of a motor vehicle while there is liquor in his body.

3

Mandatory Motor Vehicle Insurance

Financial responsibility for drivers

Arizona has financial responsibility laws. These laws require that all motor vehicles be minimally insured and that vehicle owners provide proof of insurance to law enforcement officers. Violation of Arizona's financial responsibility laws may lead to the imposition of fines and suspension of the person's driver license, vehicle registration, and license plates.

Motor Vehicle Liability Policy Requirements

Every motor vehicle operated on a highway in Arizona must be covered by a liability policy with coverage limits not less than $15,000 because of bodily injury to or death of one person in any one accident; $30,000 because of bodily injury to or death of two or more persons in any one accident, subject to the $15,000 limit for one person; and $10,000 because of injury to or destruction of someone else's property in any one accident. (These minimum policy limits are often referred to as 15/ 30/10.) Additional coverages or higher limits may be obtained,[1] but the financial responsibility laws require only the minimum coverages stated. In some cases, motor vehicles may be covered by self-insurance plans or alternate methods of coverage, but a discussion of those is beyond the scope of this chapter.

Proof of Insurance

On the investigation of a traffic accident or traffic law violation, the officer will do two things: 1) he will check the Department of Transportation's computer system to determine if there is a notice of insurance cancellation or nonrenewal, or an indication that the vehicle is not registered, and 2) he will require the driver to produce proof of financial responsibility for the vehicle. If the Department reports that there is a notice of cancellation or nonrenewal applicable to the vehicle, or that the vehicle is not registered, the officer will issue a traffic citation to the driver for one or both violations. If the driver does not produce evidence of financial responsibility to the officer, the officer will also issue a civil traffic citation to the driver. Evidence of financial responsibility may be an insurance identification card or a binder for insurance coverage.

A citation issued for failure to produce proof of insurance will be dismissed if, prior to the court date, the person produces evidence to the court that the financial responsibility requirements were met at the time the citation was issued.

Fines and Suspension Periods

A person who does not have the required insurance coverages may be fined, and his driver license, vehicle registration and license plates may be suspended. For the first violation, the court will impose a minimum penalty of $500 and, on receipt of the court record, the Department of Transportation will suspend the person's driver license, vehicle registration and license plates for three months. For a second violation within 36 months, the minimum penalty increases to $750, and the suspension period increases to six months. For a third and subsequent violation within 36 months (indicating this person is chronically uninsured), 1) the minimum penalty increases to $1,000, and the suspension period increases to one year; and 2) the Department will require on reinstatement of the driver license, the registration and the license plates, that the person provide proof of financial responsibility.

The court may reduce or waive the penalty imposed for not having the required insurance coverages, if the person subject to the penalty presents to the court proof that: 1) the person has not been found responsible for a similar violation within the past 24 months or more than one violation within the past 36 months, and 2) the person has purchased a six-month policy of insurance.

For a second and subsequent violation of the financial responsibility laws within 36 months, the judge is required to order the surrender of the person's driver license and direct the Department to suspend the person's driver license, vehicle registration and license plates for the time previously stated.

Restricted License and Registration Following Suspension

A person whose driver license, vehicle registration and license plates have been suspended may apply to the Department of Transportation for a restricted license and registration. The license and registration are restricted to travel during the course of employment, between the person's place of employment and residence, or between the person's place of residence and school. The Department will not issue a restricted license or registration until the person provides proof of financial responsibility.

4

Use of Seat Belts & Motorcycle Helmets

"Better be safe than sorry."—Proverb

Under Arizona law, a person transporting a child who is under five years of age must use a passenger restraint system; each front seat passenger and every passenger under 16 years of age must wear a safety belt; and a motorcycle rider under 18 years of age must wear a protective helmet. Regardless of the legal requirements, common sense and good judgment tell us that we should be as safe as possible whenever operating a motor vehicle. In this chapter, we will look at the legal consequences of not using safety devices (whether legally required or not).

Child Passenger Restraint System

Except in limited circumstances, it is illegal for a person to operate a motor vehicle in Arizona when transporting a child who is under five years of age, unless that child is properly secured in a child passenger restraint system. This requirement does *not* apply to: 1) a person who operates a vehicle that was originally manufactured without passenger restraint devices; 2) a person operating a recreational vehicle; 3) a person transporting a child in an emergency situation; or 4) a person who is transporting more than one child under five years of age and cannot secure them all.

If a police officer stops a vehicle for apparent violation of this law, the officer must determine *from the driver* whether the unrestrained child or children are less than five years of age. If the information given to the officer indicates that no violation of this law has occurred, the officer cannot detain the vehicle any further unless some additional violation is involved. The officer is not permitted to search or seize the vehicle during the stop, unless there is probable cause for another violation of law.

A person who violates the child restraint law is subject to a penalty of $50.

Adult Vehicle Restraints

Each front seat occupant of a moving vehicle that is designed for carrying 10 or fewer passengers must use either a lap and shoulder belt or, in older vehicles not so equipped, a lap belt. This requirement applies to all vehicles manufactured after 1971 (1972 was the first model year in which federal law made safety belts required equipment). The driver must require each passenger less than 16 years of age to wear his or her safety belt, regardless of seating position.

A police officer is not allowed to stop or issue a citation to a person operating a vehicle in violation of this law, unless the officer has reasonable cause to believe there is another violation of law. A person who violates the seat belt law is subject to a maximum penalty of $10 for each violation.

Motorcycle Helmets

The operator of a motorcycle must wear protective glasses, goggles, or a transparent face shield, unless the motorcycle is equipped with a windshield (in which case nothing else is required). If an operator or passenger is less than 18 years of age, he must wear a protective helmet. An adult operator or passenger is not by law required to wear a helmet.

Civil Mitigation Rules

Lest the wrong conclusions be drawn from the above discussion, let us now look at the mitigation rules that apply in civil cases involving motor vehicle accidents (a motorcycle is considered a motor vehicle).

Simply stated, a person who is injured in an accident cannot recover damages for avoidable consequences. Accordingly, if the non-use of a seat belt or motorcycle helmet enhanced the injuries or caused injuries which otherwise would not have occurred, the jury will be permitted to reduce the injured person's damages accordingly. This is true even if wearing a seat belt or motorcycle helmet was not required by law.

Seat Belts Save Lives

According to the National Highway Transportation Safety Administration, about 43,000 people are killed in fatal car accidents each year in the United States. Safety belts can prevent death in about half of these accidents. Wearing a seat belt is still the single most effective thing we can do to avoid traffic injuries and death. Time to buckle up!

5

Leaving the Scene of an Accident

"ACCIDENT n. An inevitable occurrence due to the action of immutable natural laws." — Ambrose Bierce

Accidents Involving Death or Injuries

The driver of a vehicle involved in an accident resulting in injury or death must immediately stop his vehicle at the scene of the accident, or as close to the accident scene as possible and immediately return to the scene.

The driver must remain at the scene of the accident until he has given certain required information and has rendered reasonable assistance to any person injured in the accident. The driver must give his name and address and the registration number of the vehicle he was driving. On request, the driver must show his driver license to the person struck or to the driver or occupants of the vehicle collided with. The driver must also make arrangements for the carrying of an injured person to a physician, surgeon, or hospital for medical or surgical treatment if it is apparent that treatment is necessary, or if the transportation is requested by the injured person.

The driver must give notice of the accident immediately by the quickest means of communication (by cell phone, if possible), to the proper law enforcement agency. The law enforcement officer who investigates the accident will prepare a written accident report.

Accidents Involving Only Damage to a Vehicle

The driver of a vehicle involved in an accident resulting only in damage to a vehicle that is driven must immediately stop at the scene of the accident, or as close to the accident scene as possible and immediately return to the scene. The driver must remain at the accident scene until he has given the required information to the other driver (see discussion above). The stop must be made without obstructing traffic more than is necessary.

If the vehicle struck is unattended (*e.g.*, in a parking lot), the driver must immediately stop and either: 1) locate and notify the operator or owner of his name and address, and the name and address of the owner of his vehicle, or 2) leave a note containing that information in a conspicuous place on the vehicle that was struck.

Failure to Stop

If a driver fails to stop and fulfill his legal obligations at the scene of an accident involving death or personal injuries, he is guilty of a felony. If he fails to stop and fulfill his legal obligations at the scene of an accident involving only property damage, he is guilty of a misdemeanor. In either case, failure to stop at the scene of an accident is a criminal offense, punishable by jail time and/or a fine.

In addition to the criminal penalties, a driver may lose his driving privileges for failing to stop and fulfill his legal obligations. The Department of Transportation will revoke the driving privileges, for five years, of a driver convicted of failing to stop at the scene of an accident involving death or serious physical injury, and for three years of a driver convicted of failing to stop at the scene of an accident resulting in an injury other than death or serious physical injury. In a case involving only property damage, the court may order the Department to suspend his license for one year.

6

Failure to Control Speed and Failure to Yield Right-of-Way

*"The Law is the true embodiment of everything that's excellent.
It has no kind of fault or flaw, ..." —* W. S. Gilbert

Drivers who fail to control their speed and drivers who fail to yield the right-of-way cause the majority of Arizona's traffic accidents. For safety's sake, it is important to understand Arizona's "rules of the road."

Reasonable and Prudent Speed

A person is prohibited from driving a vehicle on a highway at a speed greater than is "reasonable and prudent under the circumstances, conditions and actual and potential hazards then existing." He must control the speed of his vehicle "as necessary to avoid colliding with any object, person, vehicle or other conveyances on, ... the highway." The quoted language is directly from the traffic statute.

The statute sets forth the general rule that a vehicle's maximum speed must be reasonable and prudent. If speed limits are posted, they govern maximum speed. If a driver is unable to control his speed to avoid colliding with a pedestrian, bicyclist, or other vehicle or object, he will be guilty of violating Arizona's speed statute.

Right-of-Way

There are several Arizona statutes which govern right-of way. In this section, we are concerned with the two that are most often violated by drivers who cause traffic accidents. The statutes are set forth below.

Vehicle at Intersection

When two vehicles enter or approach an intersection from different streets or highways at approximately the same time, the driver of the vehicle on the left must yield the right-of-way to the vehicle on the right. (This rule does not apply to vehicles approaching or entering an uncontrolled "T" intersection if the vehicle on the left is on a continuing street or highway and the vehicle on the right is on the terminating street or highway. In those situations, the vehicle on the terminating street or highway must yield to the vehicle on the continuing street or highway.)

Vehicle Turning Left at Intersection

The driver of a vehicle within an intersection intending to turn to the left must yield the right-of-way to a vehicle that is approaching from the opposite direction and that is within the intersection or so close to the intersection as to constitute an immediate hazard. Unfortunately, this statute is often violated, resulting in serious injuries or death.

If a person violates one of the above statutes and is involved in an accident, he may be found negligent in a civil lawsuit for damages by reason of that violation. He will also have to pay a civil traffic fine, and will have points assessed against his driving record. All good reasons to obey the rules of the road!

7

Defensive Driving School

A way to avoid points for a moving violation

A person who is ticketed for a civil traffic moving violation may attend a defensive driving school. The benefits of going to "driving school" are discussed below.

Who is Eligible?

To be eligible for driving school, a person must have received a *civil* traffic moving violation, and not have been involved in an accident resulting in death or serious physical injury. A person is eligible to attend driving school one time every 24 months.

The court *may* permit a person *criminally* charged with violation of the excessive speed statute to attend driving school. This is the only exception to the rule that eligibility is limited to civil traffic moving violations. The holder of a commercial driver license or a driver of a commercial motor vehicle that requires a commercial driver license is not eligible for the defensive driving diversion program.

If a person commits a criminal traffic violation (other than as noted in the preceding paragraph) or is involved in an accident resulting in death or serious physical injury, the court may require the person to attend driving school *in addition to* another sentence imposed for the traffic violation.

A person who is eligible to attend driving school or who

has been ordered to attend by the court, must attend a supreme court certified defensive driving school within the time limit set by the court.

Fees

A person who elects to attend a driving school must pay a "court diversion fee" set by the presiding judge of each court, and a $45 surcharge. Payment of the court diversion fee and surcharge is in lieu of payment of a penalty or fine and surcharge for a traffic violation.

In addition to the court diversion fee and surcharge, a person must pay the fee to attend the driving school, and a fee of $15 for deposit in the Defensive Driving School Fund administered by the Arizona Supreme Court. All of the fees will be collected by the driving school.

The Benefits of Driving School

The court will, upon successful completion of the course, dismiss the traffic citation for which the person attended the school. In addition, the Department of Transportation will not include a record of the traffic citation on the person's driving record. However, dismissal of a traffic citation for attending traffic school does not prohibit the use of evidence pertaining to the citation in a civil or criminal proceeding.

By electing to attend defensive driving school, a person may save money on car insurance, will avoid unnecessary points on his driving record, and may even become a better driver. Not a bad deal!

8

Pool Safety

"Two seconds is too long." —Pool safety awareness slogan

Each year, nationwide, about 300 children under five years of age drown in swimming pools, according to the U.S. Consumer Product Safety Commission. In addition, more than 2,000 children in that age group are treated annually in hospital emergency rooms for submersion injuries. In Arizona, drowning is the leading cause of accidental death to children under five. In response to these tragic statistics, pool barrier laws have been enacted by the Arizona State Legislature and by cities and towns across Arizona. In this chapter, we will examine the state law regulating pool enclosures.

Under state law, a swimming pool (or other contained body of water intended for swimming that is 18 inches deep and wider than eight feet) must be entirely enclosed by at least a five-foot wall, fence or other barrier. The enclosure requirement applies to below-ground and above-ground pools alike.

The wall, fence or barrier can have no openings through which a spherical object four inches in diameter can pass. The horizontal components of the pool enclosure must be spaced not less than 45 inches apart measured vertically, or must be placed on the pool side of the wall, fence or barrier which cannot have any opening greater than one and three-quarter inches measured horizontally. Wire mesh or chain-link fences must have a maximum mesh size of one and three-quarter inches measured horizontally.

Gates for the enclosure must be self-closing and self-latching, and open outward from the pool. The law imposes height and other restrictions on the latch, which vary according to the location of the latch relative to the pool.

The wall, fence or barrier must not contain any openings, handholds or footholds accessible from the exterior side that could be used to climb the enclosure. The wall, fence or barrier must be at least 20 inches from the water's edge.

If a house constitutes part of the enclosure required by law, then: 1) there must be a minimum four-foot wall, fence or barrier between the swimming pool and the house; or 2) the pool must be protected by a motorized safety pool cover which requires the operation of a key switch and meets other standards; or 3) all ground-level doors with direct access to the pool must be equipped with self-latching devices, and windows must be equipped with latching devices, screwed in place wire mesh screens, or keyed locks, depending on their purpose and location; or 4) if the pool is above ground, it must have non-climbable exterior sides at least four feet high and any access ladder or steps must be removed and safely secured.

The pool enclosure requirements under state law do not apply to pools constructed before the enactment of the statute (June 2, 1991), to public or semi-public swimming pools, or to a residence in which all residents are at least six years of age.

Every swimming pool contractor and pool seller in Arizona is required to give the buyer or renter a notice explaining safety education and responsibilities of pool ownership.

A person who violates Arizona's pool enclosure law is guilty of a petty offense. No fine will be imposed, however, if the person installs the required pool enclosures within 45 days of the citation and attends a pool safety course.

Legal Tip:

Many cities and towns also have swimming pool barrier requirements. These requirements vary from place to place, and may be more stringent than state law. Every pool owner is advised to check his local pool barrier ordinance to ensure compliance.

Gun Laws

"The right to bear arms"

Guns are part of the rich history of the West. Cowboys, peace officers, and bandits of yester-year all carried guns--albeit for different reasons. In Arizona, the rule still is that an adult may, under most circumstances, possess and carry a gun. There are certain exceptions to this rule, however. This chapter examines those exceptions and the state laws that govern gun ownership and use.

Misconduct Involving Weapons

The law prohibits certain conduct involving weapons. Generally, a person may not legally do any of the following:

- Carry a firearm concealed on his person or within his immediate control in a vehicle (a) in the furtherance of a serious offense, a violent crime, or any other felony offense; (b) and fail, when contacted by a law enforcement officer, to accurately answer the officer if the officer asks whether the person is carrying a concealed deadly weapon; or (c) if the person is under 21 years of age.
- Manufacture, possess, transport, sell or transfer an automatic weapon, or certain short-barreled rifles and shotguns.
- Possess a firearm if the person (a) has been found to

constitute a danger to himself or to others; (b) has been convicted of a felony and his civil right to possess or carry a gun has not been restored; (c) is serving a term of imprisonment; (d) is serving a term of probation pursuant to a conviction for domestic violence or a felony offense, parole, community supervision, work furlough, home arrest or release on any other basis or is serving a term of probation or parole pursuant to the interstate compact; or (e) is an undocumented or a nonimmigrant alien.

- Sell or transfer a gun to someone who is prohibited from possessing it.
- Deface a firearm or possess a firearm knowing it was defaced.
- Use or possess a gun during the commission of a felony.
- Discharge a firearm at an occupied structure to assist, promote or further the interests of a criminal street gang, criminal syndicate or racketeering enterprise.
- Enter a public establishment or attend a public event and carry a gun after a reasonable request by the establishment operator or event sponsor to remove the weapon and place it in his temporary custody.
- Enter an election polling place on Election Day carrying a gun.
- Possess a gun on school grounds.
- Enter a nuclear or hydroelectric generating station carrying a gun.
- Supply, sell or give a gun to another person if the person knows (or has reason to know) that the other person would use the gun to commit a felony.
- Use or possess a gun in furtherance of terrorism.

There are numerous exceptions to the above-listed exceptions. In addition, many of the words and phrases used in the law have been defined by the Legislature. Accordingly, the reader is advised to consult the statute itself, A.R.S. Section 13-3102, for complete details on the subject. Misconduct involving weapons under this statute may be either a felony or a misdemeanor, depending on the particular offense.

Concealed Weapons

A permit is no longer required to carry a concealed weapon. In 2010, Arizona became just the third state in the country to allow a concealed weapon to be carried without a permit. Of course, as discussed above, the person must still be 21 years of age or older, and not otherwise prohibited from carrying a concealed weapon.

A firearm is *not* considered concealed if it is carried in: (a) a manner where any portion of the firearm or holster in which it is carried is visible; (b) a holster that is at least partially visible; (c) a scabbard or case designed for carrying weapons that is at least partially visible; (d) luggage; or (e) a case, holster, scabbard, pack or luggage that is carried within a vehicle or within a storage compartment, map pocket, trunk or glove compartment of a vehicle.

Firearm Purchases in Other States

An Arizona resident may lawfully purchase firearms anywhere in the United States if the purchase fully complies with the laws of Arizona and the state in which the purchase is made and the purchaser and seller have complied with the requirements of the federal gun control act.

Discharge of Firearms

A person may lawfully discharge a firearm: 1) on a properly supervised range; 2) in a recognized hunting area; 3) for the control of nuisance wildlife (with a permit); 4) using blanks; 5) more than one mile from an occupied structure; or 6) in self-defense (or defense of another) against a serious animal attack. It is unlawful to discharge a firearm within any Arizona city or town, except by special permit of the chief of police.

The firearm discharge rules do not apply to peace officers and animal control officers in the performance of their duties.

Local Rules

Political subdivisions of the state, e.g., counties, cities and towns, are permitted to enact laws relating to firearms, so long as those laws do not conflict with state laws. A political subdivision may enact laws prohibiting a minor from possessing or carrying a firearm under certain circumstances, regulating its employees and independent contractors within the scope and course of their employment, and limiting or prohibiting the discharge of firearms in parks and preserves.

Minors

The general rule is that a person who is under eighteen years of age and unaccompanied by a parent, grandparent or guardian, or a certified hunter safety instructor or certified firearms safety instructor is prohibited from knowingly carrying or possessing a firearm in any public place or on non-family owned or leased property. This rule does not apply to emancipated minors, or to minors who are at least fourteen years of age and who are engaged in lawful hunting or shooting events or marksmanship activities, or activities requiring the use of a firearm that are related to the production of certain agricultural products.

If a minor is apprehended for unlawful possession of a firearm, the peace officer must seize the firearm. If the parent or guardian found responsible for violating this law knew (or reasonably should have known) of the minor's unlawful conduct and made no effort to prohibit it, the parent or guardian will be responsible for any court-imposed fine and for any damages resulting from the minor's unlawful use of the firearm.

Generally, a person who sells or gives to a minor, without the consent of the parent or legal guardian, a firearm, ammunition or toy pistol by which dangerous and explosive substances can be discharged is guilty of a felony.

10

Cruelty to Animals

"Animals are such agreeable friends—they ask no questions, they pass no criticisms." —George Eliot (Mary Ann Evans)

Throwing a dog into oncoming traffic on a freeway. Starving a horse to death. Leaving newborn kittens on the street. These are all cases of animal cruelty that have been reported in the media. Arizona law makes cruelty to animals a crime.

A person may be guilty of cruelty to animals if he subjects an animal to cruel neglect or abandonment; fails to provide medical attention necessary to prevent protracted suffering; inflicts unnecessary physical injury on an animal; subjects an animal to cruel mistreatment; kills or harms an animal without the owner's consent; leaves an animal unattended and confined in a motor vehicle where physical injury or death is likely to result; allows a dog to kill or injure a service animal; or exerts unauthorized control over a service animal. An "animal" is defined by law as a mammal, bird, reptile or amphibian.

It is not cruelty to animals to expose poison to a dog that has killed or wounded livestock or to other predatory animals on property owned by the person seeking to protect himself, or his livestock or poultry. A warning notice in such cases must be posted on the property. A person may also use poisons on his property to control rodents, excluding any fur-bearing animals.

The law does not prohibit normal hunting activities, or

activities regulated by the Arizona Game and Fish Department or the Arizona Department of Agriculture.

In cases involving cruelty to animals, the state must generally prove that the person charged acted intentionally, knowingly or recklessly. A person who violates the state's cruelty to animals law is guilty of either a felony or a misdemeanor, depending on the nature of the cruel acts. In addition, any city, town or county is allowed to adopt an ordinance with misdemeanor provisions for cruelty to animals. A person found guilty of cruelty to animals under state law or a local ordinance may be sentenced to jail and/or fined, and may be required to pay damages to the owner of the animal.

11

Injunction Against Harassment

"Prevention is better than cure." —Proverb

An injunction may be issued by a court to prevent a person from committing acts of harassment. "Harassment" means a series of acts over a period of time that are directed at a specific person and that would cause a reasonable person to be seriously alarmed, annoyed or harassed, and the conduct in fact seriously alarms, annoys or harasses the person and serves no legitimate purpose.

To obtain an injunction against harassment,[2] a person must file a verified petition with a magistrate, justice of the peace, or superior court judge. Any court in Arizona may issue or enforce an injunction against harassment. No fee will be charged for filing the petition.

The petition must contain certain information about the party who is filing it (the plaintiff), as well as the party against whom the injunction is sought (the defendant). It must also include a specific statement showing events and dates of the acts constituting the alleged harassment.

The court will review the petition and any evidence offered by the plaintiff, including evidence of harassment by electronic contact or communication, to determine whether an injunction against harassment should be issued without a further hearing. If the court finds reasonable evidence of harassment of the plaintiff by the defendant within the past year, it will issue an

before any disposition of the case and to be informed of the disposition.

- To read pre-sentence reports relating to the crime against the victim when they are available to the defendant.
- To receive prompt restitution from the person or persons convicted of the criminal conduct that caused the victim's loss or injury.
- To be heard at any proceeding when any post-conviction release from confinement is being considered.
- To a speedy trial or disposition and prompt and final conclusion of the case after the conviction and sentence.
- To have all rules governing criminal procedure and the admissibility of evidence in all criminal proceedings protect victims' rights.
- To be informed of victims' constitutional rights.

The Victims' Bill of Rights is set forth in Section 2.1 of the Constitution of the State of Arizona, and is embodied in Sections 13-4401 through 13-4440 of the Arizona Criminal Code. The texts of both the Constitution and Criminal Code can be obtained at most public libraries in Arizona, or online at the Arizona State Legislature's Web site, www.azleg.gov.

13

Right to Jury Trial

"The right of trial by jury shall remain inviolate."
—Constitution of Arizona

The Arizona Constitution guarantees the right of trial by jury, in both criminal and civil cases. The right to trial by jury is a fundamental right in our democracy. The law governing jury trials in Arizona is discussed below.

Juries in Criminal Cases

A jury for trial of a criminal case in which a sentence of death or imprisonment for 30 years or more is possible will consist of 12 people. A jury for trial in the superior court of *any other* criminal case will consist of eight people. A jury for trial in a municipal or justice court will consist of six people. Regardless of the number of jurors, a verdict in a criminal case must always be unanimous.

(Every criminal case is prosecuted in the name of the State of Arizona. The prosecutor may be an assistant attorney general, assistant county attorney, or assistant city attorney.)

Juries in Civil Cases

A civil case is one in which a non-criminal matter is at issue. (For a detailed discussion about civil cases, please refer to Chapter 60.)

A jury for trial in the superior court of a civil case will consist of eight people. The vote of all but two jurors is necessary for a verdict in the superior court. In a justice court, a civil jury will consist of six people, and the vote of all but one is necessary to render a verdict. The parties may agree to a greater or lesser number of jurors, and to change the number of votes necessary for a verdict. Thus, in a civil case in the superior court, the parties might agree to a jury of nine people, and that seven votes (out of nine) will be necessary for a verdict.

Demand for Jury Trial

In some less serious criminal cases and in all civil cases, a party must make demand for a trial by jury. Depending on the type of case, there are different deadlines by which the jury trial demand must be made. If a party fails to timely demand a trial by jury (by waiting until the time of trial, for instance), he waives the right to a jury trial. In those cases, the judge will serve as the jury.

Not all cases or issues are triable of right by jury. For example, a divorce case is not eligible for trial by jury, and the enforceability of a restrictive covenant (discussed in Chapter 94) will be determined by the judge and not a jury. Cases involving certain non-serious crimes, such as leaving the scene of an accident (discussed in Chapter 5) or filing a false report, are also not eligible for trial by jury. In some cases, some issues may be tried to a jury, and others tried to the judge. The party seeking trial by jury must specify which issues in the case he wants tried to a jury.

Most often, in a civil case a jury will determine questions of fact (*e.g.*, which party was at fault), and the judge will decide questions of law (*e.g.*, which documents should be considered by the jury in determining fault). A jury is not allowed to consider questions of law, but in the absence of a jury, the judge will determine all questions of fact (in addition to questions of law).

The parties may voluntarily waive their right to trial by jury in both civil and criminal cases. In a serious criminal case, however, the permission of the judge is needed for an accused to waive this important constitutional right.

14

Jury Duty

"All qualified jurors have an obligation to serve on juries when summoned by the courts..." —Policy of Arizona

If a person is at least 18 years of age and is registered to vote or has a driver license, his name undoubtedly is on a list of eligible juror candidates.

A master jury list is maintained by the jury commissioner of every county. At least twice a year, the names of prospective jurors to serve on trial and grand juries are selected at random from the master jury list. The jury commissioner then mails a questionnaire to each person whose name was drawn from the master jury list to determine his qualifications to serve, and whether he has valid grounds to be excused from service.

If a person's answers to the jury questionnaire indicate that he is disqualified for jury service or state grounds sufficient to be excused from jury service, he will be excused. If the jury commissioner refuses to excuse a person who claims he is disqualified or is entitled to be excused, that person may ask the presiding judge to decide whether he should be excused.

A prospective juror who is at least 75 years of age may submit a written statement to the court requesting that he be excused from service. On receipt of the request, the judge or jury commissioner will excuse the prospective juror from service.

A person may be summoned to serve on a trial jury in

federal district court, the superior court, a justice court, or a municipal court, or to serve on a federal, state or county grand jury. The manner in which a person is summoned for jury duty may be different in each case. In the superior court, the jury summons is generally mailed to a person at his place of residence.

If a person fails to appear in response to a jury summons, a second summons will be sent. Failure to respond to the second summons may lead to the person's arrest and a fine of up to $500.

A person who is scheduled to appear for jury duty may postpone the date of his initial appearance only twice. To postpone an appearance, the person summoned must contact the jury commissioner and request a postponement.

An employer may not discipline or fire an employee for fulfilling his jury service obligation.

According to statistics published by the Maricopa County Superior Court, more than half a million jury summonses are mailed every year for all of the courts within the county limits, and for the state and county grand juries. Only a small fraction of the people who receive jury summonses are actually sworn as jurors. A person who has been summoned and selected to serve on a jury in Arizona is generally not required to serve again as a juror for two years.

Those sworn as jurors in the superior court are entitled to a jury fee of $12 per day plus mileage to and from the courthouse. A juror whose service lasts more than five days may submit a request for payment from the Arizona Lengthy Trial Fund. The amount of replacement or supplemental earnings paid will be at least $40 but not more than $300 per day beginning on the fourth day of service. The amount a juror receives from the Fund is limited to the difference between the jury fee paid to the juror and the juror's actual lost earnings, up to $300 per day. Jurors who are unemployed are eligible to be paid $40 per day.

Despite the inconvenience, jury service is still both a duty and a privilege.

15

Arizona Notaries Public

*A Notary Public is a public officer commissioned by the
Secretary of State to perform notarial acts.*

Becoming a Notary

To become a notary public in Arizona, a person must meet
the following requirements:

- Be an Arizona resident.
- Be at least 18 years old.
- Be a citizen or legal permanent resident of the United States.
- Not have been convicted of a felony (unless civil rights have been restored).
- Not have had an Arizona notary commission revoked within past four years.

A person interested in becoming a notary must complete a
notary public application and purchase a four-year $5,000 bond
in duplicate form from an insurance agent. The completed
application and notary bond must be submitted to the Arizona
Secretary of State, together with a filing fee in the amount of
$43. If the applicant meets the requirements to become a notary
public, the applicant will be commissioned as a notary public
and the Secretary of State will issue to the applicant a commission certificate. A commission certificate is a person's proof
that he has been commissioned as a notary public.

A notary public commission is valid for four years. There is no automatic renewal process for a commission; it is the notary's responsibility to initiate the renewal process. A notary should submit a renewal application, new bond and filing fees to the Secretary of State's office 60 days before the expiration of his commission. A notary public may continue to notarize until midnight of the expiration date of his current commission. A notary public who chooses to allow a commission to expire must deliver his notary public seal, notary public journal, and other notary records to the Secretary of State's office.

Performing Notarial Acts

Once a commission certificate is issued, the notary must purchase a notary seal and a notary journal. A notary is required by law to authenticate all of his official acts with a seal, and to record all of his notarial acts (in chronological order) in a journal. The duties of a notary public can only be performed when he has an original commission certificate, a notary bond, a notary public seal, and a notary public journal. In addition, each notary is required to have a copy of the *Arizona Notary Public Reference Manual* published by the Arizona Secretary of State.

It is necessary to notarize documents to prevent fraud, to prove the authenticity of the signature, and to prove the signature was made willingly. There are four notarial acts that a notary can perform in Arizona: 1) acknowledgements, 2) jurats, 3) copy certifications, and 4) oaths or affirmations. Each type of notarial act is explained below.

Acknowledgement: the notary certifies that a signer, whose identity is personally known to the notary or is proven by satisfactory evidence, voluntarily signs a document for its stated purpose. The signer is not required to sign the document in the notary's presence; however, the document cannot be signed at a later time.

Jurat: the notary certifies that a signer, whose identity is personally known or is proven by satisfactory evidence, has made in the notary's presence a voluntary signature and has taken an oath or affirmation vouching for the truthfulness of the signed document.

Copy certification: the notary certifies that he has made a photocopy of an original document that is neither a public record nor publicly recordable.

Oath or affirmation: a person makes a vow in the presence of the notary under penalty of perjury, with reference to a supreme being in the case of an oath.

A notary is an impartial witness. An impartial witness must have no conflict of interest. This means that a notary cannot be a party to the transaction or a party to the document, and a notary cannot have any financial or beneficial interest in the transaction. The law prohibits a notary from performing notarial services for anyone related to him by marriage or adoption (but given the impartiality requirements, a better practice would be to not notarize for *any* family member).

A notary is commissioned in the county of his residence, but he may perform notarial acts throughout the state of Arizona. An Arizona notary may not, however, notarize documents outside the state of Arizona.

A notary may charge a fee for performing notarial acts, but he can charge no more than $2 per transaction. The maximum fee for each notarial act is set by law. A notary must post in a conspicuous place a schedule of fees that he is allowed to charge. A notary is, of course, free to charge a fee less than allowed by law, or to waive a fee entirely.

For more information and an application form, the reader should contact the Arizona Secretary of State. The contact information is set forth below:

Arizona Secretary of State
1700 W. Washington, 7th Floor
Phoenix, AZ 85007-2888
Attention: Notary Section
Phone: (602) 542-4758
Fax: (602) 542-4366
Web site: www.azsos.gov

PART TWO

Consumer Laws

16
Consumer Fraud

"It contains a misleading impression, not a lie. I was being economical with the truth." —Robert Armstrong

Consumer fraud in Arizona is illegal. Consumer fraud is defined as any deception, deceptive act or practice, false pretense, false promise or misrepresentation made by a seller or advertiser of *merchandise*. Concealment, suppression or failure to disclose a material fact also is consumer fraud if it is done with the intent that others rely on the factual omission. "Merchandise" means objects, wares, goods, commodities, intangibles, real estate or services.

A victim of consumer fraud may file a complaint with the Arizona Attorney General's Office. If it appears to the Attorney General that a person or company has engaged or is engaging in consumer fraud, he may obtain from the superior court an injunction prohibiting that person or company from continuing the unlawful activity. The court may also enter an order to restore to a consumer fraud victim any monies or property which were acquired by unlawful means. A consumer complaint form can be obtained by contacting the Office of the Attorney General, telephone (602) 542-5763 (Phoenix), (520) 628-6504 (Tucson), or (800) 352-8431; www.azag.gov/consumer/complaintformintro.html. A complaint can also be filed online at the Attorney General's Web site.

If a court finds that a person or company has willfully

violated the consumer fraud laws, the Attorney General may recover from the violator, on behalf of the state, a penalty of up to $10,000 per violation.

The consumer fraud laws do not apply to owners or publishers of newspapers or magazines which print advertisements, or to the owners or operators of radio or television stations which broadcast advertisements, when the owner, publisher or operator has no knowledge of the intent, design or purpose of the advertiser.

The consumer fraud laws also create a private cause of action for consumer fraud victims. Thus, a victim of consumer fraud may bring a lawsuit against the person or company guilty of consumer fraud for money damages. The lawsuit must be brought within one year from the date the claim arises.

17

Lemon Law

Turning lemons into lemonade

A "lemon" is a new vehicle that cannot be repaired after numerous attempts. The Arizona Lemon Law requires the manufacturer of a lemon to replace or repurchase the vehicle. To take advantage of the Lemon Law, a new vehicle owner first must report the problem to the manufacturer and give the manufacturer a reasonable opportunity to repair the vehicle. The process to turn a lemon into lemonade is discussed below.

Reporting the Defect

Each new vehicle comes with express warranties. The manufacturer, for instance, will warrant that the drive train will function properly for a stated period of time. The Lemon Law ties into these express warranties. If a new vehicle does not conform to an express warranty, the owner must report the nonconformity to the manufacturer, its agent or its authorized dealer or issuer of a warranty. The report must be made during the term of the express warranty or within two years or 24,000 miles following the date of original delivery, whichever is earlier. The manufacturer is required to make those repairs that are necessary to conform the vehicle to the express warranties, even if the repairs are made after the expiration of the warranty term or two-year period or 24,000-mile limit.

Repair Attempts

If the manufacturer is unable to conform the vehicle to the express warranty by repairing or correcting a defect or condition which substantially impairs the use and value of the vehicle after *a reasonable number of attempts,* the manufacturer must either repurchase or replace the vehicle with a new vehicle. It is presumed that a reasonable number of attempts have been made if the same defect or condition has been subject to repair four or more times by the manufacturer during the shorter of the express warranty term or the period of two years or 24,000 miles following the date of original delivery, whichever is earlier, or the vehicle is out of service by reason of repair for a total of 30 or more days during that time period. The presumption does not apply, however, against a manufacturer unless it has received prior written notification of the defect from the owner and it has had an opportunity to fix the problem.

Replacement or Repurchase

If the manufacturer repurchases the vehicle, it will refund to the owner the full purchase price, including all collateral charges (sales tax and license fees), less a reasonable allowance for the owner's use of the vehicle. The manufacturer must make refunds to the owner and any lienholder, as their interests appear. A reasonable allowance for use does not include any period when the vehicle was out of service for repairs.

If the manufacturer replaces the vehicle with a new vehicle of *lesser* value, it must refund to the owner the difference between the original amount of sales tax and the amount of sales tax attributed to the replacement vehicle. If the manufacturer replaces the vehicle with a new vehicle of *greater* value, additional sales tax will be payable.

A manufacturer will not be required to replace or repurchase a vehicle in cases where the nonconformity does not substantially impair the use and market value of the vehicle, or the nonconformity is the result of abuse, neglect or unauthorized modifications or alterations of the vehicle.

Lawsuit Against Manufacturer

If the manufacturer has established or participates in an informal settlement procedure, the owner must participate in such a procedure before the provisions relating to refunds or replacement will apply. The owner of a lemon must file a lawsuit within six months following the earlier of expiration of the express warranty term or two years or 24,000 miles following the date of original delivery, whichever is earlier. If the owner wins the case, the court will award him reasonable costs and attorney's fees.

A manufacturer who has replaced or repurchased a vehicle because it is a lemon must, before offering the vehicle for resale, attach to the vehicle written notification that it has been replaced or repurchased.

In that manufacturers have agents and authorized dealers through whom they conduct business, any reference in this chapter to the manufacturer generally includes its agents and its authorized dealers.

18

Bad Checks

Bad checks mean bad news.

Writing bad checks is a crime, and may also subject the bad-check writer to a lawsuit for twice the amount of the check. This chapter deals with the crime of bad-check writing and the separate civil action for money damages.

The Criminal Component

Bad-check writing is classified as theft in the Arizona Criminal Code. A person is guilty of bad-check writing if he issues a check knowing that he does not have sufficient funds on deposit with the bank for the payment in full of the check "as well as all other checks outstanding at the time of issuance." There are three defenses to bad-check writing: 1) the payee was notified in advance that the check writer did not have sufficient funds on deposit to ensure payment of the check; 2) the check is postdated and sufficient funds are on deposit on the later date for payment of the check; and 3) insufficiency of funds resulted from an adjustment to the check writer's account by the bank without notice to him.

If payment is refused by the bank on which the check is drawn within 30 days after the check is issued, the person to whom the check was issued may send a notice of dishonored check to the check writer, requiring payment of the check amount, plus reasonable costs and protest fees. The check writer has 12 days from his receipt of the notice to remit full payment to the check holder. If payment in full is not made within that time, the holder of the check may turn the matter over to the county attorney for criminal prosecution.

Except as provided in the next paragraph, issuing a bad check is a class 1 misdemeanor. A class 1 misdemeanor is punishable by up to six months in jail and a fine of up to $2,500.

Issuing a bad check in the amount of $5,000 or more is a class 6 felony if the check writer fails to pay the full amount of the check, including accrued interest at the rate of 12% per year and any other fees provided by law, within 60 days after receiving notice of the dishonored check. A class 6 felony is punishable by up to one and a half years in prison and a fine of up to $250,000.

The county attorney in each county is responsible for prosecuting bad-check cases. In Arizona's two most populated counties, Maricopa and Pima, the county attorneys have developed quite useful Web sites for victims of bad checks. In Maricopa County, go to www.maricopacountyattorney.org to view information or to download submittal forms from the *Check Enforcement Guidebook*. In Pima County, go to www.pcao. pima.gov/badcheck.htm for information about its bad check program and to obtain forms and guides. A visitor to either Web site will be able to download a Bad Check Guidebook and all the forms needed to submit a dishonored check to that county attorney's bad-check program.

The Civil Component

A bad-check writer may also be liable for civil damages. The statute creating the civil action says that a person who, with intent to defraud, gives to another person a check, knowing at the time of delivery that he does not have an account or does not have sufficient funds in his account to pay the check in full, is liable to the holder of the check for twice the amount of the check, or $50, *whichever is greater*, together with costs and attorney's fees.

To establish liability under this section, the holder of the check must give the check writer notice of nonpayment and afford him 12 days to pay the check. The notice of nonpayment may be given to the check writer in person or in writing. Written notice is recommended. Notice in writing must be given by certified mail, return receipt requested, to the person at his address as it appears on the check.

A lawsuit under this section must be filed within one year.

19

Door-to-Door Sales

"The buyer may cancel a home solicitation sale until midnight of the third business day after the sale agreement is signed."

In legal parlance, a door-to-door sale is called a "home solicitation sale." Home solicitation sales are strictly regulated in Arizona. The statutes governing home solicitation sales contain important consumer rights. This chapter explains those legal rights.

Definition of Home Solicitation Sale

A home solicitation sale is a sale of goods or services in which the seller personally solicits the sale at the buyer's home (or the home of a friend), and some part of the purchase price is payable in installments. A cash sale will be deemed a home solicitation sale if the seller makes a loan to the buyer or assists in obtaining a loan for the buyer to pay the purchase price.

A sale is *not* a home solicitation sale if: 1) it is pursuant to a pre-existing account with a business that sells goods or services at a fixed location, or 2) it is a sale made pursuant to prior negotiations between the parties at a business establishment where the goods or services are offered for sale.

Requirements of a Home Solicitation Sale Contract

To be effective, a home solicitation sales contract must be written in the same language used in the oral sales presentation, and be accompanied by a notice of cancellation form. The agreement must also be dated, signed by the buyer, and include certain consumer rights information. The statute spells out the exact language that must be included in the agreement. (The text of the statute, A.R.S. Section 44-5004, may be downloaded from the Arizona State Legislature's Web site, www. azleg.gov.)

Cancellation of Home Solicitation Sale

The buyer may cancel a home solicitation sale until midnight of the third business day after the sale agreement is signed. In counting business days, Sundays and certain federal holidays are not included.

Cancellation of the contract occurs when the buyer gives written notice of cancellation. The seller is required by law to furnish a cancellation notice form to the buyer at the time of the sale. The cancellation notice must be given to the seller in person, by telegram or by mail. (The author recommends giving written notice by registered mail.) The cancellation notice must be sent to the seller at the address provided by him. Any provision of a contract or agreement that waives a buyer's right of cancellation is void and has no effect.

In some cases, a buyer may not cancel a home solicitation sale if he requested the seller to provide goods or services without delay because of an emergency.

Steps Required After Cancellation

The seller must return to the buyer any payments, promissory notes, or goods traded in, within 10 days after a home solicitation sale has been cancelled. If the seller fails to return traded-in goods within the 10-day period, the buyer may recover an amount equal to the trade in allowance for the goods stated in the agreement.

The buyer may retain the seller's goods until the seller has complied with his obligation to return payments, evidence of indebtedness, and traded-in goods. The law gives the buyer a lien on the goods for any recovery to which he is entitled, until the seller has complied with his obligations.

Except as provided above, within 20 days after a home solicitation sale has been cancelled, the buyer upon demand must return to the seller any goods delivered by the seller pursuant to the sale. The buyer is not required to tender the goods at any place other than his own address. If the seller fails to take possession of the goods within 20 days after cancellation, the goods will become the property of the buyer without any obligation to pay for them.

If the seller has performed any services pursuant to a home solicitation sale prior to its cancellation, the seller is entitled to a cancellation fee of 5% of the cash price, $15, or the amount of the cash down payment, *whichever is less*. If the seller's services result in the alteration of the buyer's property, the seller must restore the property to substantially as good condition as it was in at the time the services were rendered.

Legal Tip:

A person who has entered into a home solicitation sale contract and wants to cancel it should read the language of the contract carefully. Every home solicitation sale contract is required by law to contain a notice of cancellation provision. The person should be sure to give written notice of cancellation to the seller (preferably by registered mail) by no later than midnight of the third business day after the sale agreement is signed.

20

Motor Vehicle Repair Liens

"If the owner fails to pay the charges, the repair facility may sell the vehicle."

Lien for Unpaid Charges

Owners and operators of garages and repair and service stations by law have a lien upon motor vehicles for labor, materials, supplies and storage for the amount of the charges, when the amount of the charges is agreed to by the repair facility and the vehicle owner. The motor vehicle repair lien does not affect any other lien on the vehicle.

Sale of Vehicle

When possession of the vehicle has continued for 20 days after the charges accrue and remain unpaid, the repair facility may notify the owner (if in the county where the vehicle is located) to pay the charges. If the owner fails to pay the charges within 10 days after notice is given, the repair facility may sell the vehicle at public auction and apply the proceeds to payment of the charges. The balance of the proceeds must be paid to the owner (or other person entitled to the money). If the vehicle owner does not reside in the county where the vehicle is located, the repair facility is not required to give the 10 days' notice to pay before proceeding to sell.

Five days' notice of sale must be given to the owner if he can be found. If the owner cannot be found, the notice of sale must be published twice in a newspaper published in the county.

If the person entitled to the balance is unknown or has left the county, the balance will be paid to the Arizona Department of Revenue. If the balance is not claimed by the person entitled to the money within two years, the unclaimed money will be deposited in the permanent state school fund.

21

Residential Landlord-Tenant Act

The relationships of residential landlords and tenants in Arizona is controlled by the Arizona Residential Landlord and Tenant Act.

In Arizona, the rental of "dwelling units" is controlled by the Arizona Residential Landlord and Tenant Act. The Act does not apply to the rental of non-residential property, such as commercial and industrial real estate, or to transient occupancy in a hotel or motel. This chapter looks at some of the rights and obligations of residential landlords and tenants under the Act.

Landlord's Obligations

The landlord, at the beginning of the rental term, must disclose to the tenant in writing of the name and address of the manager of the property, and the owner of the property or his agent for purposes of service of process and receiving notices and demands. This information must be kept current. The landlord must inform the tenant in writing that the Arizona Residential Landlord and Tenant Act is available on the Secretary of State's Web site. Where there is a written rental agreement, the landlord must provide a signed copy to the tenant (and the tenant must sign and deliver to the landlord one fully executed copy).

A landlord may not discriminate. It is illegal, for example, to refuse to rent to people with children, unless there is another legal basis for the refusal.

A landlord also is obligated to:

- Comply with the requirements of building codes materially affecting health and safety.
- Make all repairs and do whatever is necessary to keep the premises in a fit and livable condition.
- Keep all common areas in a clean and safe condition.
- Maintain in good and safe working order all electrical, plumbing, sanitary, heating, ventilating, air conditioning and other facilities and appliances supplied by him.
- Provide receptacles for the removal of ashes, garbage, rubbish and other waste, and arrange for their removal.
- Supply running water and reasonable amounts of hot water, and reasonable heat and air conditioning or cooling where those units are available.

Tenant's Rights

If a landlord breaches one or more of his obligations, the tenant may deliver a written notice to the landlord specifying the facts of the breach. If the noncompliance involves health and safety, the notice must state that the rental agreement will terminate on a date not less than five days after receipt of the notice, if the breach is not remedied within five days. For any other significant breach, the time period to terminate the rental agreement and to remedy the breach cannot be less than 10 days.

If the landlord remedies the breach within the time limit stated in the tenant's notice, the tenant may not terminate the rental agreement. If the landlord fails to remedy the breach and the tenant elects to terminate the rental agreement, the tenant may sue the landlord for damages caused by the wrongful eviction.

Domestic Violence

A tenant may terminate a rental agreement if the tenant provides to the landlord written notice that the tenant is the victim of domestic violence. The tenant's rights and obligations under the rental agreement are terminated and the tenant must vacate the dwelling if the tenant provides written notice requesting release from the agreement with a mutually agreed upon release date within the next 30 days, accompanied by a copy of a protective order showing the tenant is the victim of domestic violence, or a police report stating that the tenant notified the law enforcement agency that the tenant was a victim of domestic violence. Early termination by a tenant for domestic violence is only permitted, however, if the events that resulted in the tenant being a victim of domestic violence occurred within the 30-day period immediately preceding the written notice of termination.

A tenant who is a victim of domestic violence may require the landlord to install a new lock to the dwelling if the tenant pays for the cost of installing the new lock.

Tenant's Self-Help

When a landlord fails to comply with his obligation to maintain the premises *and* the cost of repair is less than $300 or an amount equal to one-half of the monthly rent, whichever is greater, the tenant may notify the landlord in writing of his intent to correct the condition. If, after being notified by the tenant, the landlord fails to comply within 10 days or as promptly thereafter as conditions require in case of emergency, the tenant may have the work done by a licensed contractor. The tenant must deliver to the landlord an itemized statement and a lien waiver from the contractor, and then may deduct the cost of the work from his rent.

When a landlord fails to supply essential services, hot or cold water, heat, or air conditioning (where the units are installed or offered), the tenant, after giving reasonable notice to the landlord, may obtain the missing essential services and deduct the cost from the rent, recover damages from the land-lord, or obtain substitute housing during the period of the landlord's noncompliance and be excused from paying rent.

Tenant's Obligations

A tenant is required to:

- Maintain the dwelling unit in a clean and safe condition.
- Use utilities and other facilities in a reasonable manner.
- Not deliberately or negligently destroy or deface the premises.
- Conduct himself in a manner that will not disturb his neighbor's peaceful enjoyment of the premises.
- Pay his rent on time.
- Use and occupy the premises only as a dwelling unit, unless otherwise agreed.
- Allow the landlord reasonable access to the dwelling unit to inspect the premises, make repairs, decorations, alterations, or improvements, supply services, or to show the property to third parties.

Landlord's Rights

If the tenant fails to pay rent, the landlord may give five days' written notice of his intention to terminate the rental agreement. If rent is not paid within the five days, the landlord may terminate the rental agreement and sue the tenant for possession of the premises. A court action for possession is called a "special detainer" action. The landlord may also bring a claim for damages for breach of the rental agreement.

Anytime prior to the entry of a judgment in a special detainer action for non-payment of rent, the tenant may reinstate the rental agreement by paying to the landlord the unpaid rent, late fees, and the landlord's attorney fees and costs. If the tenant is found guilty of special detainer, the landlord will be granted possession of the premises, late charges, fees and costs, and unpaid rent.

The landlord may immediately terminate a rental agreement for a tenant's serious misconduct. Serious misconduct includes, but is not limited to, illegal discharge of a firearm, criminal street gang activity, illegal drug activity, assault, or any serious property damage. In a special detainer action for serious misconduct, the court will set a trial date within three business days from the filing of the complaint and, if the court finds that serious misconduct did occur, it will grant the landlord the return of the premises within 24 hours.

A landlord may also terminate a rental agreement for a tenant's noncompliance with the terms of the agreement. To terminate a rental agreement for noncompliance, the landlord must first give the tenant an opportunity to remedy the breach. If the noncompliance affects health and safety, the tenant will be given five days to remedy the breach; otherwise, the tenant will be given 10 days to do so.

If a tenant fails to maintain the premises, and the noncompliance can be remedied by repair, replacement, or cleaning, the landlord has the right of self-help. Except in cases of emergency, the landlord is required to give 14 days' notice of the breach and request that the tenant make the repairs. If the tenant fails to do so, the landlord may enter the dwelling and perform the work or hire it done in a workmanlike manner. The landlord can then submit an itemized bill for the reasonable value or actual costs of the work, which must be paid by the tenant as additional rent. There is no limit to the landlord's cost of repairs.

Security Deposits

A landlord is prohibited from demanding or receiving security, however denominated, including prepaid rent, in excess of one and one-half month's rent. A tenant is not, however, prohibited from voluntarily paying more than one and one-half month's rent in advance. A landlord may charge, in addition to a security deposit, nonrefundable fees for cleaning and redecorating. The purpose of all nonrefundable fees or deposits must be stated in writing by the landlord. The landlord does not have to account for nonrefundable fees at the termination of the rental agreement.

At the end of the rental period, the security deposit may be applied to unpaid rent and damages caused by the tenant. The landlord has a duty to account to the tenant for prepaid rent and security. Within 14 business days after the tenant's demand (following termination of the tenancy), the landlord is required to provide a written itemized statement of charges, and to return the unused portion of the security deposit to the tenant. Failure by the landlord to comply with this provision will allow the tenant to sue for any amounts wrongfully withheld by the landlord as security, plus damages equal to twice the amount wrongfully withheld.

Legal Tip:

Persons interested in this topic may download the Arizona Residential Landlord and Tenant Act from the Arizona Secretary of State's Web site, www.azsos.gov.

22

Arizona's Homestead Exemption

A homestead exemption protects $150,000 equity in a person's dwelling from attachment, execution and forced sale.

A homestead means a dwelling in which a person resides. The dwelling may be a house, condominium, or mobile home. A person's homestead is exempt from attachment, execution and forced sale by creditors, up to $150,000. Here are the rules pertaining to the state's homestead exemption.

The Basic Rules

The homestead exemption is available to any adult (18 or over) who resides within the state. Only one homestead may be held by a married couple or a single person. The value of the homestead refers to the *equity* of a single person or married couple. Equity is calculated by subtracting all liens and encumbrances from the fair market value of the homestead property.

Illustration: If the fair market value of the homestead property is $350,000 and the mortgage balance is $200,000, the value of the homestead, or equity, is $150,000.

If a married couple lived together in a homestead property and are then divorced, the total exemption allowed for that residence to either or both persons cannot exceed $150,000 in value.

A homestead property may be any one of the following: 1) property in one compact body upon which exists a dwelling house, 2) one condominium or cooperative, 3) a mobile home, or 4) a mobile home plus the land on which it is located. The key is that the person claiming the homestead must reside in the structure to which the exemption applies.

If a homestead property is sold, the exemption automatically attaches to the sale proceeds, up to the value permitted by law (see above discussion). The homestead exemption in identifiable cash proceeds continues for 18 months after the sale of the property or until the person establishes a new homestead with the proceeds, whichever period is shorter. A person may hold only one homestead exemption at a time.

Other Rules

A person who is entitled to a homestead exemption holds the exemption by operation of law and no written claim or recording is required. (Under prior law, a declaration of homestead had to be recorded. This is no longer required.)

If a person has more than one property to which a homestead exemption could reasonably apply, a creditor may require the person to designate which property is protected by the homestead exemption. In those cases, the debtor must designate the property by recording a homestead exemption in the office of the county recorder where the property is located or by sending the creditor a certified letter, return receipt requested, within 30 days after receiving the creditor's demand letter.

A person's homestead is exempt from process and from sale under a judgment or lien, except: 1) a consensual lien (such as a mortgage or deed of trust), 2) a mechanic's or materialman's lien, 3) a lien for child support arrearages or spousal maintenance arrearages, or 4) to the extent that a judgment or other lien may be satisfied from the equity of the debtor *exceeding* the homestead exemption (*i.e.*, equity in excess of $150,000).

Illustration: A person contracts to have work done on his homestead, and a mechanic's lien is legally filed against the property for an unpaid balance. Regardless of the homestead exemption, the property will *not* be exempt from foreclosure of the lien.

A homestead may be abandoned by a declaration of abandonment or waiver, a transfer of the homestead property, or a permanent removal of the person from the residence or the state. A person may remove from the homestead for up to two years without abandonment or a waiver of the exemption.

The transfer of homestead property into a living trust does not constitute an abandonment of the homestead, so long as the person retains the power to administer and revoke the trust (see Chapter 45 for a detailed discussion of revocable trusts).

Homestead laws vary from state to state. Arizona's homestead laws provide substantial protection to homeowners against the claims of creditors.

23

Personal Property Exemptions

"Exempt personal property cannot be taken from its owner, even in bankruptcy."

Personal property used for personal, family or household use may be exempt from execution, attachment, garnishment, replevin, sale, or any other debt collection process. The personal property discussed in this chapter is shielded by law from the claims of creditors, and may not be taken by legal process to satisfy any debt. If a person files bankruptcy, this property is also exempt from the claims of creditors in the bankruptcy proceeding.

In the case of a married couple, each spouse is entitled to the exemptions listed below, which may be combined with the other spouse's exemption in the same property or taken in different exempt property.

Household Furniture, Furnishings and Appliances

A person's basic household furniture, furnishings and appliances are generally exempt from process, provided their aggregate fair market value does not exceed $4,000. The specific items of household furniture, furnishings and appliances are listed in the governing statute, A.R.S. Section 33-1123.[1]

Food, Fuel and Provisions

All food, fuel and provisions actually provided for in a person's individual or family use for six months are exempt from process.

Personal Items

The following personal items are exempt from process (the value listed for each category is aggregate fair market value):

- Wearing apparel not in excess of $500.
- Musical instruments not in excess of $250.
- Domestic pets and animals not in excess of $500.
- Engagement and wedding rings not in excess of $1,000.
- A library not in excess of $250.
- A watch not in excess of $100.
- A typewriter, bicycle, sewing machine, family bible, burial lot, and a firearm (shotgun, rifle or pistol) not in excess of $500.
- A motor vehicle not in excess of $5,000 (if a person is physically disabled, this exemption increases to $10,000).
- Any professionally prescribed prostheses for a person or his dependent.

Money Benefits or Proceeds

Certain money benefits and proceeds are exempt from the claims of creditors (except for child support debts). The complete list is set forth in A.R.S. Section 33-1126. The protected benefits and proceeds are summarized below:

- A spouse's or parent's life insurance proceeds, not exceeding $20,000.
- A minor child's earnings.
- Child support or spousal maintenance.
- Proceeds or benefits from any employer-sponsored health, accident or disability insurance (certain exceptions apply).

- Proceeds from insurance on any exempt property that is destroyed or damaged.
- The cash surrender value of life insurance policies owned at least two years (certain exceptions apply).
- An annuity contract owned at least two years (certain exceptions apply).
- Damages recoverable for levy or sale of exempt property, or the wrongful taking or detention of exempt property.
- $150 in a bank or credit union account.
- A person's interest in a retirement plan or deferred compensation plan (certain exceptions apply).
- For a person who does not exercise the homestead exemption (see the preceding chapter on Arizona's homestead exemption), prepaid rent and security deposits, not exceeding the lesser of $1,000 or one and one-half months' rent.

School Equipment

School equipment that is used by a person for the instruction of youth in any university, college, seminary of learning or school is exempt, irrespective of value.

Tools and Equipment

The tools and equipment of a person used in a commercial activity, trade, business or profession, not in excess of $2,500, are generally exempt from process. Farm machinery, utensils, implements of husbandry, feed seed, grain and animals, not in excess of $2,500, belonging to someone whose primary income is derived from farming, are exempt. All arms and uniforms required to be kept by a person, irrespective of value, are exempt.

Wages and Salary

The maximum amount of a person's disposable earnings (net income) for any workweek which is subject to process (i.e., garnishment) may not exceed 25% of the disposable earnings for that week, or the amount by which disposable earnings exceed 30 times the minimum federal hourly wage, whichever is less. These wage and salary exemptions do not apply in the case of an order for child support or spousal maintenance (in which case, only one-half of the disposable earnings are exempt), in the case of a Chapter 13 bankruptcy proceeding (also called a wage-earners plan or reorganization), or for any tax debt.

24

Good Samaritan Laws

"Nothing can harm a good man, either in life or after death."
—Socrates

A Good Samaritan Law is generally defined as one that limits the liability of licensed doctors and nurses who voluntarily render care at the scene of an accident. In Arizona, there are also laws that limit the liability of physicians who volunteer at amateur athletic events, and of people who donate and distribute food items and grocery products to those in need. This chapter explains the liability exemptions that are given to Arizona's Good Samaritans and volunteers under those laws.

Emergency Care

Any licensed health care provider, ambulance attendant, driver, pilot, or any other person who, gratuitously and in good faith, renders emergency care at a public gathering or at the scene of an emergency occurrence is not liable for ordinary negligence. (The law of negligence is discussed in Chapter 62.) A health care provider or other person rendering emergency aid is, however, still liable for gross negligence.[2]

A licensed or certified health care provider who gratuitously and in good faith renders emergency health care within his scope of practice, to an athlete injured during an amateur athletic practice or event, is not liable for ordinary negligence. The health care provider is still liable for gross negligence,

73

however. This law applies to health care providers who agree to voluntarily attend amateur athletic practices, contests and events to be available to render emergency health care.

Food and Grocery Products

A person who makes a good faith donation of a food item or a nonfood grocery product to a charitable or nonprofit organization is not liable for damages for injury or death due to the condition of the donated food item or grocery product.

The food item must appear to be intended for human consumption and meet all applicable quality and labeling standards. The nonfood grocery product must appear to meet all applicable quality and labeling standards.

If the food item or nonfood grocery item does not comply with all quality and labeling standards imposed by law, the donor must so inform the charitable or nonprofit organization, and the organization must agree to recondition the donation to comply with those standards before its distribution.

A donor of a food item or grocery product who complies with these rules is liable for damages only if the injury or death is a direct result of his intentional misconduct or gross negligence. Similar exemptions apply to charitable and nonprofit organizations, and their employees and volunteers who in good faith receive and distribute without charge the donated food items and nonfood grocery products.

25

Unlicensed Contractors

Contracting without a license is a crime.

It is illegal for a commercial or residential builder to conduct business in Arizona without first obtaining an appropriate contractor's license.[3] In this chapter, we will examine the licensing requirements and some situations in which a license is not required. We will also look at the consequences of engaging in contracting without a license.

"Contractor" is synonymous with the term "builder." It means any person or company that, for compensation, directly or indirectly constructs, alters, repairs, adds to, subtracts from, improves, moves, wrecks or demolishes any building, road, railroad, excavation or other structure, project development or improvement.

Also included within the definition of contracting is: 1) the erection of scaffolding or any other structure or work in connection with the construction, 2) connecting a structure or improvements to utility service lines and metering devices and the sewer line, and 3) providing mechanical or structural services for any structure or improvement.

The term contractor includes subcontractors, specialty contractors, floor covering contractors, landscape contractors (other than gardeners), and project managers and consultants.

A "residential contractor" is the same as a residential builder, and generally means anyone who works on residential structures, such as houses, townhouses, condominiums, cooperative units, and apartment complexes of four units or less.

Exemptions to Licensing Requirements

There are 16 separate exemptions to the licensing requirements. They are set forth in A.R.S. Section 32-1121(A). (The statute may be downloaded from the Arizona State Legislature's Web site, www.azleg.gov.) The most common exemptions are listed below:

- A property owner who improves his property or builds structures on his property for occupancy solely by him and his family. To qualify for this exemption, the owner-builder cannot offer to rent or sell the structure for one year after completion or issuance of a certificate of occupancy.
- A supplier of finished products, materials or articles of merchandise who does not install or attach the items (unless the value is $1,000 or less).
- A person who sells or installs certain electrical fixtures and appliances, regardless of the value.
- A property owner who is acting as a developer and who builds a structure on his property for sale or rent *and* who contracts for the project with a properly licensed contractor. The licensed contractor's name and license number must be included in all sales documents.
- A gardener who performs lawn, garden, shrub and tree maintenance.
- A person engaging in work for which the total contract price, including all labor and materials, but excluding certain electrical fixtures and appliances, is less than $1,000. Under this exemption, the work must be of a casual or minor nature, and the person must disclose in any advertising that he is "not a licensed contractor."

Penalties for Violation

Acting in the capacity of a contractor without a license is a class 1 misdemeanor. For the first offense, an unlicensed contractor will be fined not less than $1,000. For the second and any subsequent offense, the minimum fine is $2,000.

In addition, an unlicensed contractor is prohibited from collecting any monies owed under a construction contract. In order to maintain a civil action to collect compensation, the contractor must prove that he was licensed when the contract was entered into and when the claim arose.

Licensing Information

As shown above, anyone engaging in contracting activities within the state of Arizona, whether as a commercial or residential contractor, unless exempt, must obtain a license from the Arizona Registrar of Contractors. Contractor information and forms may be obtained from the Registrar of Contractor's Web site, www.azroc.gov.

Any consumer who is harmed by a contractor, whether or not the contractor is licensed, should promptly report the matter to the Registrar of Contractors. The Registrar of Contractors may be reached by calling (602) 542-1525, or toll free outside Maricopa County within Arizona, (877) 692-9762.

26

Residential Contractors' Recovery Fund

"Licensed contractors build confidence." —Licensed Contractors' Slogan

The Arizona Registrar of Contractors administers a recovery fund for the benefit of homeowners who have been damaged by licensed residential contractors. The fund is known as the Residential Contractors' Recovery Fund. In this chapter, we will see how the Fund works and who may benefit from it.

Every residential contractor must contribute money to the Fund when applying for a license or upon renewal of a license. The Fund was established for the protection of any owner of residential real property which is actually occupied or intended to be occupied by the owner. It also protects some renters and homeowners' associations.

The Fund is not available to a homeowner who deals with an unlicensed contractor, or with a contractor whose license was in an inactive status, expired, cancelled, revoked, suspended or not issued at the time of the contract. (For a discussion concerning Arizona's licensing requirements, please refer to the preceding chapter on unlicensed contractors.)

Recovery Fund Limits

A homeowner may not recover more than $30,000 from the Fund for any one claim, irrespective of the actual amount of damages. The liability of the Fund is limited to $200,000 for any one residential contractor's license. The claims from the Fund are paid in the order of the date of entry of the payment orders. In other words—first come, first served. No further recovery from the Fund will be allowed after the sum of $200,000 has been paid from it, for any one contractor.

An award from the Fund is limited to the actual damages suffered by a homeowner as a result of a contractor's failure to adequately build or improve a residential structure. The amount awarded will not exceed the actual cost of completing or repairing the structure. If a homeowner has paid a deposit or down payment and no actual work was performed or materials delivered, the award will be the amount of the deposit or down payment plus interest at the rate of 10% per annum from the date the deposit or down payment was made, not to exceed $30,000.

Lawsuit Procedure

To collect from the Fund, a homeowner may file a lawsuit against the contractor in the superior court or in justice court, depending on the amount of the claim. (For information regarding Arizona's justice courts, please refer to Chapter 82.) The lawsuit must be filed within two years from the date of the commission of the act that was the cause of the injury or from the date of the occupancy.

When a homeowner files a lawsuit which may result in payment from the Fund, he must notify the Registrar of Contractors in writing to that effect. The Registrar may intervene in the suit and defend the claim. If the contractor has a bond from which recovery may be had, the homeowner should join the bonding company in the lawsuit. A homeowner must attempt to collect from all possible sources of recovery, including a bond covering the contractor, before payment from the Fund will be allowed.

If a homeowner is awarded a judgment against the contractor, he may apply to the court for an order directing payment out of the Fund. To obtain this order, the homeowner must show that he has given the required notices to the Registrar, that the judgment is final, that he has proceeded against any bond, and that he is unaware of any property or assets of the contractor which could be used to satisfy the judgment. If the homeowner has recovered a portion of his loss from other sources, only the unpaid amount may be collected from the Fund.

Administrative Procedure

If a contractor's license has been revoked or suspended because the contactor refuses or is unable to comply with an order of the Registrar to remedy a violation, the Registrar may order payment from the Fund to the injured homeowner, without the need for the homeowner to file a lawsuit against the contractor.

The Registrar will require, in addition to a completed claim form, three complete itemized written bids from properly licensed residential contractors for repairs or completion of the work originally contracted for, copies of contracts and cancelled checks, front and back. A copy of the escrow settlement should be included with claims covering new residential construction.

Bankruptcy by Contractor

If a contractor files bankruptcy, the homeowner must ask the bankruptcy court for permission to make a claim against the Fund. Until such permission is given, a homeowner may not proceed with a recovery fund claim.

For additional information concerning the Residential Contractors' Recovery Fund, the reader is advised to contact the Registrar of Contractors, or visit its Web site, www.azroc.gov.

27

Real Estate Recovery Fund

"We was robbed!" — Joe Jacobs, U.S. Boxing Manager

If you have been harmed by a salesperson or broker in a real estate or cemetery transaction, you may be eligible for payment from the Real Estate Recovery Fund.

The Fund is administered under the direction of the Arizona Real Estate Commissioner, for the benefit of any person who has been injured by the misconduct of a licensed real estate or cemetery salesperson or broker. The money in the Fund comes from a surcharge on real estate license fees.

The Fund is liable to pay for damages arising out of a transaction in which the salesperson or broker performed acts for which a license was required, *or* when the salesperson or broker, while acting as the principal in the purchase or sale of real property, engaged in fraud or misrepresentation *and* someone was harmed due to reliance on the salesperson's or broker's licensed status.

The Department of Real Estate offers the following examples of losses that are covered by the Fund:

- Misappropriated earnest money deposit or down payment on a house.
- Misappropriated security deposit, rental income, or money withheld that was intended for mortgage payments or other expenses managed by the salesperson or broker.

- Repair costs required for defects when a salesperson or broker materially misrepresented the condition of the property.
- Loss caused in a transaction when the salesperson or broker actively misrepresented the financial condition of the property and parties involved.

To get paid from the Fund, a person must file a lawsuit against the salesperson or broker, and all other persons who may be responsible for the loss. The lawsuit cannot be started later than five years from the accrual of the cause of action. If a person obtains a judgment against a salesperson or broker for prohibited conduct, that person may apply to the Recovery Fund Administrator for payment from the Fund. The payment application must be made within two years after the termination of all proceedings, reviews and appeals connected with the judgment.

The Department of Real Estate will supply the payment application form that includes detailed instructions with respect to the information and documents that are necessary for payment. The Recovery Fund Application may be downloaded from the Department's Web site, www.azre.gov. The completed application and supporting documents should be hand-delivered or sent by certified mail to the Recovery Fund Administrator at:

Department of Real Estate
2910 North 44th Street, Suite 110
Phoenix, AZ 85018

The person submitting the application (sometimes referred to as the "claimant") must also mail a copy to the salesperson or broker, together with a notice form that should be supplied by the Department.

A claimant will be entitled to recover from the Fund the money actually lost in the real estate or cemetery transaction, including reasonable attorney's fees and costs, but he must deduct the value of any property recovered, payments, settlement amounts, insurance proceeds, tax benefits or deductions, or other offsets. Prior to getting paid from the Fund, a claimant will be required to show that he exhausted all attempts to collect the lost money from the salesperson or broker, and any other person responsible for the loss.

The Fund's liability is limited to $30,000 per transaction, or $90,000 per license. The spouse of a salesperson or broker cannot file a claim.

The Commissioner is generally required to make a decision on a claim within 90 days after receiving a completed application for payment. If the application is approved, payment will be made on the claim. If it is denied, the claimant may pursue the application in court. To do so, he must file a verified application in the court within six months after receiving notice of the denial. Other procedural rules also apply to the appeal process.

If a payment is made from the Fund, the licenses and license rights of the responsible salesperson or broker will be terminated.

For more information, the reader may wish to contact the Recovery Fund Administrator, recovery_fund@azre.gov, or visit the Department of Real Estate's Web site, www.azre.gov.

PART THREE

Family Law

28

Prenuptial Agreements

"The legality of love"

Wine and roses...and prenuptials. While a premarital agreement is not appropriate in every case, one may be appropriate where one spouse has children by a prior marriage or where the spouses, for whatever reason, wish to provide in advance of marriage for the disposition of their property upon separation, divorce, or death.

Premarital agreements have not always been favored in Arizona. In fact, at one time, a contract before marriage providing that the husband would be relieved from the burden of supporting his wife in the event of divorce would have been contrary to public policy and, thus, unenforceable. The law has changed, however, and premarital agreements are no longer against public policy. Arizona, with a majority of other states, has adopted the Uniform Premarital Agreement Act, which, as the name implies, governs the scope and enforceability of premarital agreements.

Prospective spouses are now free to enter into an agreement in contemplation of marriage, which will be effective on marriage. A premarital agreement must be in writing and signed by both parties. The agreement is enforceable without consideration.

Scope of Premarital Agreements

The parties to a premarital agreement may contract with respect to a wide variety of issues, including:

- The rights and obligations of each of the parties in any of the property of either or both of them, including income and earnings;
- The right to buy, sell or use any property or assets during marriage;
- The disposition of property on separation, divorce, death, or any other event;
- The modification or elimination of spousal support (alimony);
- The making of a will or trust to carry out the provisions of the agreement; and
- The ownership of life insurance policies.

The parties may contract with respect to any other matter not listed above, so long as the provision is not in violation of a public policy or a statute imposing a criminal penalty. The right of a child to support may not be adversely affected by a premarital agreement.

Enforcement of Premarital Agreements

A premarital agreement is not enforceable if the person against whom enforcement is sought proves:

- The person did not execute the agreement voluntarily; or
- The agreement was unconscionable (grossly one-sided) when it was executed and before execution of the agreement that person:
  - » Was not provided a fair and reasonable disclosure of the property or financial obligations of the other party.
  - » Did not voluntarily and expressly waive, in writing, any right to disclosure of the property or fi-

nancial obligations of the other party beyond the disclosure provided.

» Did not have, or reasonably could not have had, an adequate knowledge of the property or financial obligations of the other party.

The law contains an exception for modification or elimination of spousal maintenance. If a provision of a premarital agreement modifies or eliminates spousal support and that modification or elimination causes one party to be eligible for public assistance at the time of separation or divorce, the court, despite the terms of the agreement, may require payment of spousal support to alleviate the need for public support.

Legal Tips:

- Each party should fully disclose his or her assets prior to entering into a premarital agreement.
- Each party to a premarital agreement should be represented separately by legal counsel.
- Each party should retain a duplicate original of the agreement after it has been executed.

Marriage

"Marriages are made in heaven." —Proverb

1. Non-Covenant

The Arizona Legislature has declared that the purposes of marriage are to promote strong families and strong family values. There are two types of marriages in Arizona: 1) non-covenant marriage, and 2) covenant marriage. In this section, we will examine the laws relating to non-covenant marriages. Covenant marriages, which require the parties to receive pre-marital counseling and to commit in writing to take all reasonable efforts to preserve their marriage, are discussed in the next section.

Getting married in Arizona is relatively easy. There is no residency requirement. There is no waiting period. And, no tests are required. The fee for a marriage license is $72.

Not everyone may legally marry, however. The law forbids marriage between people closely related[1] and between persons of the same sex. Persons under the age of 18 may not marry without the consent of their custodial parent or guardian. Persons under 16 must also obtain the approval of an Arizona superior court judge.

A valid marriage in Arizona requires: 1) the issuance of a marriage license by the clerk of the superior court, and 2) a ceremony performed by a duly ordained or licensed clergyman, or a judge, and at which at least two adult witnesses participate. In addition, the marriage must be solemnized (entered into) before the expiration of the marriage license. The license expires one year from the date of issuance.

Illustration: The prospective bride and groom obtained a marriage license, but then postponed the wedding. They were married in a ceremony performed by their clergyman 13 months after the marriage license was issued. Because the marriage license expired before the ceremony, the marriage is not valid.

If either party to the marriage ceremony has not been divorced from a prior spouse, the marriage is invalid. A person who is legally separated may not remarry until the prior marriage is dissolved.

A marriage conducted in another state or country is valid in Arizona so long as it was valid under the laws of the place where it was contracted, with the exception of a prohibited union referenced above.

A Note About Common Law Marriages

A common law marriage is one that is not solemnized in the ordinary way (*i.e.*, non-ceremonial), but created by an agreement to marry, followed by cohabitation.

Arizona does not allow or recognize common law marriages contracted within the state, but will recognize a valid common law marriage contracted in another state. The validity of a common law marriage is determined by the laws of the state in which it was contracted.

2. *Covenant Marriage*

"Marriage is a covenant between a man and a woman who agree to live together as husband and wife for as long as they both live; ..." —Covenant Marriage Declaration

The concept of covenant marriage was first introduced in Arizona in 1998, by the adoption of the Covenant Marriage Act.[2] Persons who have the legal capacity to marry may enter into a covenant marriage by declaring their intent to do so on their application for a marriage license and by complying with the covenant marriage statutes. A declaration of intent to enter into a covenant marriage must contain certain written statements by the prospective husband and the prospective wife, including a promise to seek marital counseling if they experience marital difficulties.

The Declaration must also contain an affidavit by the parties that they have received premarital counseling from a member of the clergy or from a marriage counselor. The statute requires that premarital counseling include: 1) a discussion of the seriousness of covenant marriage; 2) communication of the fact that a covenant marriage is a commitment for life; 3) a discussion of the obligation to seek marital counseling in times of difficulties; and 4) a discussion of the exclusive grounds for legally terminating a covenant marriage by dissolution of marriage or legal separation. A notarized statement that is signed by the clergy or counselor must be submitted with the application for marriage license.

The Arizona Supreme Court has published a pamphlet entitled "Covenant Marriage in Arizona." This informational pamphlet is provided to the parties during their premarital counseling. It is also available online at: www.supreme.state. az.us/dr/Pdf/covenant.pdf.

Conversion of Existing Marriage to Covenant Marriage

An existing marriage may be converted to a covenant marriage. A husband and wife may enter into a covenant marriage by submitting to the clerk of the superior court the Declaration and a sworn statement of their names and the date and place their marriage was contracted, and by paying a filing fee. A husband and wife who apply for a covenant marriage are not required to receive premarital counseling, and they are not required to have the converted marriage separately solemnized.

Dissolution of Covenant Marriage

If a husband and wife have entered into a covenant marriage, the court cannot enter a decree of dissolution of marriage unless it finds one of the following: 1) the respondent spouse (*i.e.,* the spouse against whom the divorce is filed) has committed adultery; 2) the respondent spouse has committed a felony and has been sentenced to death or imprisonment; 3) the respondent spouse has abandoned the marital home for at least a year and refuses to return; 4) the respondent spouse has physically or sexually abused the spouse seeking the dissolution of marriage, a child, a relative living in the marital home, or has committed domestic violence or emotional abuse; 5) the spouses have been living separate and apart continuously without reconciliation for at least two years before the filing of the petition for dissolution; 6) the spouses have been living separate and apart continuously without reconciliation for at least one year from the date the decree of legal separation was entered; 7) the respondent spouse has habitually abused drugs or alcohol; or 8) the husband and wife both agree to a dissolution of marriage.

Decree of Legal Separation

If a husband and wife have entered into a covenant marriage, the court cannot enter a decree of legal separation unless it finds 1, 2, 3, 4, 5, or 7 above, or that the respondent spouse's habitual intemperance or ill treatment of the other spouse renders their living together insupportable.

By contrast to the above, if a husband and wife have *not* entered into a covenant marriage, the court may enter a decree of dissolution or a decree of legal separation upon finding that the marriage of the parties is "irretrievably broken." This finding may be based solely on the allegation of one spouse, and does not require a finding of fault by either party.

30

Community Property

"Each spouse owns an undivided and indivisible one-half interest in all community property."

Community Property Concepts

The concept of community property traces its origins to the civil laws of Mexico and Spain. When Arizona was first settled by Americans, they found Mexican and Spanish settlers already here. It is from the Mexican and Spanish settlers that the community property concept was adopted.

The law of community property exists in only nine states: Arizona, California, Idaho, Louisiana, Nevada, New Mexico, Texas, Washington, and Wisconsin. (The other 41 states have different forms of ownership concepts.) Even among the nine community property states, however, the laws relating to community property vary widely.

Community property is a theory of property ownership by the marital community itself, as opposed to ownership by either spouse individually. The foundation of the community property concept is a valid marriage. There is no community and, thus no community property, without a valid marriage. If a marriage was valid where it was contracted, so long as it is not void or prohibited under Arizona law, it is valid in Arizona.

Illustration: A man and a woman contracted a valid common law marriage in another state, and then moved to Arizona.

Even though Arizona does not allow or recognize common law marriages contracted within the state, it will recognize a valid common law marriage contracted in another state. Thus, this hypothetical couple's common law marriage will be valid in Arizona, and community property concepts will apply.

Community vs. Separate Property

Under the community property law of Arizona, each spouse owns an undivided and indivisible one-half interest in all community property. (This may be good news for some readers, who may have moved to Arizona from one of the 41 states that do not have community property laws.) The interest of each spouse remains undivided until the community is dissolved. The ways in which a community may be dissolved are discussed later in this chapter.

All property acquired by either husband or wife during the marriage, except that which is acquired by gift or inheritance, is the community property of the husband and wife. The incomes of both the husband and the wife during the marriage, in the absence of an agreement to the contrary, become community property. All property saved or purchased out of the parties' salaries or wages likewise becomes community property. Gifts to the community are also community property. The way in which property is titled does not determine whether it is community property. There is a strong presumption in the law that all property acquired during marriage is community property.

Not all property of a husband or wife is necessarily community property, however. For instance, any property owned by a spouse before marriage, as well as any property which is acquired by gift or inheritance afterward, is the *separate property* of that spouse. The income and gains from separate property are also separate property. Property that spouses agree shall be separate is separate property, and property that one spouse gives to the other intending it to be separate property is separate property. In some cases, the spouses agree in a prenuptial agreement that certain property will be separate property, even if that same property would otherwise be community property. (For a discussion concerning prenuptial agreements, please refer to Chapter 28.)

Separate property can be changed into community property by agreement, gift, or by mixing it with community property. Separate funds commingled with the community funds may lose their identity as separate property, because when commingling occurs the property is presumed to be community. In such cases, it becomes a matter of proving the nature of the property. If the separate property can be identified, commingling will have no effect.

Dissolution of the Community

The community is dissolved, and thus the community property form of ownership ceases, upon the happening of one of these three events: 1) service of a petition for dissolution of marriage, legal separation, or annulment, if the petition results in a decree; 2) the death of one spouse; or 3) the execution of a separation agreement by the spouses. The community property is divided and distributed differently in each case, as explained below.

Dissolution of marriage, legal separation, or annulment. In an action for dissolution of marriage or legal separation, the court has the power to divide the community property equitably, and to confirm to each spouse his or her separate property. The terms of the decree will control the distribution of the property. Under certain circumstances, the court may order an unequal division of the community property. In an action for annulment, by comparison, the marriage is deemed never to have existed and, accordingly, there is no community property to divide. (For a more complete treatment of this topic, please refer to Chapter 32.)

Death of a spouse. When one spouse dies, the deceased spouse's estate is made up of his one-half interest in the community property and all of his separate property. The deceased spouse's property will pass according to the terms of his will, or if he did not have a will, by the laws of intestate succession. (For the rules for determining heirs, please refer to Chapter 48.)

Agreement by the spouses. The last way to dissolve the community is by mutual agreement of the spouses. The spouses have the power to enter into a separation or property settlement agreement dividing the community property between them. Upon the execution of such an agreement, the property is owned by the spouses as separate property or in some other non-community form.

31

Marital Debts

"Neither a borrower nor a lender be." —William Shakespeare

Debts incurred after marriage are presumed to be community obligations. If the spouse creating the debt intended to benefit the community, the debt is a community obligation.

Because the foundation of community property is a valid marriage, this discussion is applicable only to married couples in Arizona. Single persons cannot own community property, nor can they incur debts for which a community may be liable. (For a discussion concerning community property, please refer to the preceding chapter.)

The general rule is that *either* spouse may contract debts and otherwise act for the benefit of the community. However, *both* spouses must join in certain transactions for the acquisition, disposition, or encumbrance of an interest in real property, and in transactions involving guaranty, indemnity, or suretyship.

Illustration #1: The husband applies for a loan that will be secured by a deed of trust on the married couple's house. Because the transaction involves an encumbrance of an interest in real estate, the joinder of both spouses in the transaction is required. This means that the transaction cannot be completed without the wife's signature.

In an action on a community debt or obligation, the spouses must be sued jointly. The debt or obligation will be satisfied first from the community property, and second, from the separate property of the spouse contracting the debt or obligation.

Illustration #2: The wife, while driving to play golf, negligently injures a pedestrian. The injured pedestrian can sue both spouses and recover from community property and, if that is inadequate, from the wife's separate property. (Of course, if the couple in this illustration is properly insured, their insurance company will pay damages to the pedestrian injured by the wife's careless driving).

If both spouses are not named as defendants in a lawsuit arising out of a community obligation, such as in the above illustration, recovery may be had only against the separate property of the spouse who committed the negligent act.

Some additional rules:

- The separate property of a spouse is not liable for the separate debts or obligations of the *other* spouse, absent agreement of the property owner to the contrary.
- The community property is liable for a spouse's debts incurred outside Arizona during the marriage that would have been community debts if incurred in this state.
- The community property is liable for the premarital separate debts of a spouse, incurred after September 1, 1973, but only to the extent of the value of that spouse's contribution to the community that would have been his separate property if single.

Debts or liabilities incurred before marriage are classified as separate, and collectible out of the separate property of the person who incurred them. However, as noted in Additional Rule #3 above, a creditor may also reach the contribution of that spouse to the community property with respect to premarital debts or liabilities incurred after September 1, 1973, in order to avoid so-called marital bankruptcy (avoidance of the premarital debt by the act of marriage).

Child Support: In a case involving child support, the court ruled that the obligation of the husband for the support of his child from a prior marriage was a premarital obligation. Accordingly, the wages of his second wife could not be reached to satisfy the child support obligation.

As noted in the preceding chapter on community property, the community is dissolved upon the happening of one of these three events: 1) service of a petition for dissolution of marriage, legal separation, or annulment, if the petition results in a decree; 2) the death of one spouse; or 3) the execution of a separation agreement by the spouses. Once the community is dissolved, the community property is not liable for subsequent debts or obligations incurred by either spouse. In the case of divorce or legal separation, the community property ceases to be liable for the individual debts of either spouse upon service of process in that action (so long as the petition results in a decree), despite the existence of a valid marriage.

In an action for dissolution of marriage or legal separation, the court has the power to allocate the community debts and obligations among the husband and the wife. Community debts not allocated by the court remain the joint obligation of the parties. However, any allocation of debts by the court is not binding on the parties' creditors; to satisfy a community debt, a creditor may pursue community property assigned to either spouse.

Illustration #3: The husband and wife have a credit card balance at the time of their divorce. The charges on the card were incurred during their marriage. The court orders the husband to pay the debt. Instead of paying the debt as ordered, the husband files bankruptcy. The credit card company can sue the wife to collect the credit card balance, and she will be unable to pursue the debt against her former husband because he is in bankruptcy.[3]

A married person who understands the law governing community debts will be better able to build and maintain good credit. Because credit is so important, every effort should be made to protect it.

32

Annulment, Dissolution and Legal Separation

"The first wife is matrimony, the second company, the third heresy." —Proverb

Sixty percent of first marriages now end in divorce, according to published statistics. For second marriages, the failure rate jumps to 70%. It is little wonder, then, that Arizona courts have seen a sharp increase in the number of family law cases in recent years.

When a marriage fails, either spouse may petition the superior court to obtain a decree of annulment, a decree of dissolution, or a decree of legal separation. (Each type of proceeding is discussed in this chapter.) A marriage may be terminated either by a decree of annulment or a decree of dissolution (commonly called a "divorce decree").[4] Dissolution proceedings are much more common than annulment proceedings, due to the difficulty in obtaining an annulment (discussed below). A decree of legal separation does not terminate the marriage, but it does terminate the spouses' community property rights and obligations.

Three Types of Proceedings

1. *Annulment.* To grant an annulment, the court must find an impediment exists that renders the marriage "null and void." Arizona statutes give little guidance on this require-

ment, but case law indicates that lack of capacity and fraudulent intent each constitute sufficient grounds for annulment. In one case, an annulment was granted where a spouse suffered from chronic alcohol abuse. In another case, an annulment was granted where a spouse suffered from manic-depressive disorder. The courts found in those cases that the conditions at issue interfered with the legal ability of the parties to enter into the marital relationship. In that annulment renders the marriage null and void, *the marriage is deemed never to have validly existed.*

2. *Dissolution.* A proceeding to dissolve a marriage, by contrast to a proceeding for annulment, presumes the existence of a valid marriage. At the conclusion of a dissolution proceeding, the once valid marriage is terminated and the husband and wife are "divorced."

3. *Legal separation.* An action for legal separation requires the same findings and results in the same orders as an action for dissolution of marriage. The difference, however, is that the marriage is not terminated. This option is typically used by persons not wanting to terminate their marriage for legal, moral or religious reasons, but still desirous of terminating their marital community. The termination of the marital community terminates the parties' community property rights and obligations.

Starting the Proceeding

In order for the court to acquire jurisdiction over a marriage, at least one spouse must have been a resident of Arizona for 90 days immediately prior to the filing of the action. A proceeding to terminate a marriage or for legal separation must be brought in the superior court in the county in which the couple resides. If one spouse resides outside the state, the action must be brought in the county in which the filing party resides.

Except in cases involving covenant marriages (discussed in Chapter 29), it is not appropriate to allege the fault of a party as a reason to terminate the marriage, only that the marriage is "irretrievably broken." If a husband and wife have entered into a covenant marriage, the court cannot enter a decree of dissolution or a decree of legal separation unless it finds the existence of one of the conditions set forth in the Covenant Marriage Act (such as adultery, imprisonment for a felony, abandonment or sexual abuse).

Cooling-off Period

In any action to terminate a marriage or for legal separation, the parties must wait at least 60 days from when service of process is completed until they can obtain the final decree. This is the statutory "cooling-off period," and is intended by the legislature to prevent a married couple from making a decision to terminate their union in the heat of marital discord. In contested cases—where the parties are disputing property division, support, custody or visitation—the time necessary to conclude the case will be much longer than the cooling-off period. The time it takes to conclude a contested family law case will depend on the pace at which the case is prosecuted and, ultimately, the trial court's calendar.

Contested Cases

The judge to whom the case is assigned decides all contested issues in a family law case. There is no right to a jury trial in Family Court.

In any of these proceedings, the court has broad power to divide and distribute property. This includes the power to impose a lien upon the separate property of a party to secure payment of child support, spousal maintenance, or any interest of the other spouse in the marital property.

Arizona law requires the Family Court judge to divide community property "equitably" between the parties. This does not necessarily mean that the division will be equal, however. Nor does the division have to be "in kind"—one spouse can be awarded certain assets and the other spouse awarded different assets. The division, nonetheless, must be a substantially equal division in the absence of a compelling reason to the contrary.

Illustration: The parties in a dissolution action own a house having a net equity value of $300,000, and a business having substantially the same value. The Family Court judge may award the house to the wife and award the business to the husband, or visa versa. This would be a substantially equal division of the assets in question, but would not be a division in kind.

Waste

Wrongful dissipation (waste) or destruction of community property by one spouse may be a reason for an unequal division, as a means of ensuring equitable treatment of the innocent spouse. Accordingly, if a spouse hides, conceals or destroys property belonging to the marital community, that spouse can expect to be awarded less than half of the remaining assets when the court divides the parties' property.

Ten Common Misconceptions About Divorce

1. **The spouse who files for divorce first has an advantage.** No. The spouse who files the divorce petition is known as the "petitioner." The other spouse is the "respondent." The petitioner has no substantive advantage over the respondent in the divorce proceedings.

2. **If my spouse has an affaire, I will be able to use evidence of the affaire to get a better settlement in my divorce case.** No. Arizona is a no-fault state. This means that evidence of marital misconduct, except to establish grounds for dissolution in a covenant marriage or to show how the conduct may affect the children for custody purposes, is irrelevant in a divorce case.

3. **If I voluntarily leave the family home while the divorce is pending, I will lose some property or custody rights.** No. It is often better for one spouse to set up a separate residence while the divorce is pending. That spouse does not lose any of his or her legal rights by doing so.

4. **If I get an order of protection, I can prevent my spouse from seeing the children.** No. An order

of protection does not cover custody or visitation rights. Only the judge in the divorce case can award custody and visitation.

5. **The judge will prefer the mother over the father in awarding child custody.** No. The judge is not allowed to consider a parent's gender when making child custody decisions. The test for child custody is always: what is in the best interests of the children?

6. **If I am awarded custody, the judge will let me live in the family home with the children until they finish high school.** Not usually. The judge may order that the family home be sold and the proceeds divided between the parties. It is often unfair to permit one spouse to live in the home for an extended period of time after the divorce, especially when the other spouse remains obligated on the mortgage.

7. **If we are awarded joint custody, the children will spend equal time with each of us.** Not necessarily. Joint custody does not necessarily mean joint *physical* custody. It is, however, the public policy of Arizona that absent evidence to the contrary, it is in a child's best interest to have substantial, frequent, meaningful and continuing parenting time with both parents.

8. **If we are awarded joint custody, neither of us will be required to pay child support to the other.** No. The court will order the payment of child support in joint custody cases, despite the fact that each parent has legal custody of the children. However, because one of the factors used to determine the amount of child support is the actual time spent by each parent with the children, the amount of child support tends to be less in a joint custody case.

9. **Alimony (spousal maintenance) is awarded to the wife in most divorce cases.** No. Spousal maintenance is *not* awarded in most divorce cases, primarily because each spouse typically is able to support

himself or herself without it. Moreover, spousal maintenance can be awarded to either the husband or the wife.

10. **If an asset is titled in my name, such as a checking account, it will be awarded to me in the divorce.** Not necessarily. The court will look to see how an asset was acquired to determine whether it is community or separate property. The way in which an account is titled is irrelevant for purposes of this determination. If an asset is acquired during the marriage, except by inheritance or gift, it will generally be deemed community property (see Chapter 30).

33

Child Custody

*Custody is awarded in accordance
with the best interests of the child.*

Child custody may be awarded in an action for dissolution of marriage, legal separation, or paternity. The court, in determining the best interests of the child in a custody proceeding, is required by law to consider all relevant factors. Those factors include:

- The wishes of the parents as to custody.
- The wishes of the child as to the custodian.
- The interaction and interrelationship of the child with his or her parents, siblings, and any other person who may significantly affect his or her best interest.
- The child's adjustment to home, school, and community.
- The mental and physical health of all persons involved.
- Which parent is more likely to allow the child frequent and meaningful contact with the other parent (not applicable if a parent is acting in good faith to protect a child from domestic violence or child abuse).
- Whether one parent, both parents, or neither parent has provided primary care of the child.

- The nature and extent of coercion or duress used by a parent in obtaining an agreement regarding custody.
- Whether a parent has complied with the provisions regarding domestic relations education.
- Whether either parent was convicted of false reporting of child abuse or neglect.
- Whether there has been domestic violence or child abuse.

In awarding child custody, the court may order sole custody or joint custody. Sole custody means that one parent has legal custody. Joint custody means that the parents share legal custody or physical custody, or both. It is the declared public policy of Arizona that absent evidence to the contrary, it is in a child's best interest: 1) to have substantial, frequent, meaningful and continuing parenting time with both parents, and 2) to have both parents participate in decision-making about the child. The law therefore favors joint custody over sole custody, absent evidence that joint custody is not in the child's best interest. The court in determining custody does not prefer a parent as custodian because of that parent's sex.

Joint Custody

The court may issue an order for joint custody of a child if both parents agree and submit a written parenting plan *and* the court finds such an order is in the best interests of the child.

The court may order joint *legal* custody without ordering joint *physical* custody. Joint legal custody means that both parents share legal custody and neither parent's rights are superior. Joint physical custody means that the physical residence of the child is shared by the parents in a manner that assures the child has substantially equal time and contact with both parents.

The court may issue an order for joint custody over the objections of one of the parents if the court believes that joint custody is in the child's best interests. Joint custody will *not* be awarded if significant domestic violence exists, or if there has been a significant history of domestic violence.

Before an award is made granting joint custody, the parents must submit to the court a proposed parenting plan. The parenting plan must include at least the following elements:

- Each parent's rights and responsibilities for the personal care of the child and for decisions in areas such as education, health care, and religious training.
- A schedule of the physical residence of the child, including holidays and school vacations.
- A procedure by which proposed changes, disputes, and alleged breaches may be mediated or resolved.
- A procedure for periodic review of the plan's terms by the parents.
- A statement that the parties understand that joint custody does not necessarily mean equal parenting time.
- A statement that each parent has read, understands, and will abide by the sex offender notification requirements.

If the parents are unable to agree on any element to be included in the parenting plan for joint custody, the court will determine that element. The court may determine other factors that are necessary to promote and protect the emotional and physical health of the child.

Access to Records

Generally, both parents are entitled to equal access to documents and other information concerning the child's education and physical, mental, moral and emotional health including medical, school, police, court and other records. Unless otherwise provided by court order or law, on reasonable request either parent may obtain the records directly from the custodian of the records or from the other parent.

Drug Offenses

If a parent has been convicted of any drug offense within 12 months before the petition or request for custody is filed, there is a presumption that sole or joint custody by that parent is not in the child's best interests.

Domestic Violence

The court will deem evidence of domestic violence as being contrary to the best interests of the child. The safety and well-being of the child and of the victim of domestic violence is of primary importance. In determining custody, the court will consider a perpetrator's history of causing or threatening to cause physical harm to another person.

If a parent seeking custody has committed an act of domestic violence against the other parent, there will be a presumption that an award of custody to the parent who committed the act of domestic violence is contrary to the child's best interests. This presumption does not apply if both parents have committed an act of domestic violence.

If a parent has committed an act of domestic violence, that parent must prove to the court's satisfaction that parenting time will not endanger the child or significantly impair the child's emotional development. In such cases, the court may order restricted or supervised contact between the parent and child, for the child's protection and well-being.

Sexual Offenders; Murders

Unless the court finds that there is no significant risk to the child, it will not grant sole or joint custody of a child or unsupervised parenting time to a parent who is a registered sex offender, or who has been convicted of first degree murder and the victim was the other parent of the child. A child's parent or custodian must immediately notify the other parent or custodian if he knows that a convicted or registered sex offender or a person who has been convicted of a dangerous crime against children may have access to the child.

Relocation of Child

If both parents are entitled to custody or parenting time and they both reside in the state, at least 60-days' advance written notice must be provided to the other parent before a parent may relocate a child outside the state or more than 100 miles within the state. The notice must be made by certified mail, return receipt requested, or pursuant to the rules of family law procedure. Within 30 days after notice is given, the other parent may petition the court to prevent the relocation of the child. The court will determine whether to allow the parent to relocate the child in accordance with the child's best interests. The burden of proving what is in the child's best interests is on the parent who is seeking to relocate the child. To the extent practicable, the court will make appropriate arrangements to ensure the continuation of a meaningful relationship between the child and both parents.

Modification of Custody Award

The court has the power to change the terms of any custody award. A parent may not, however, make a motion to modify a custody order earlier than one year after its date, unless there is reason to believe that the child's present environment may seriously endanger the child's physical, moral, or emotional health.

At any time after a joint custody order is entered, a parent may petition the court for modification of the order on the basis that domestic violence, spousal abuse or child abuse occurred since the entry of the joint custody order.

Six months after the entry of a joint custody order, a parent may petition the court for modification of the order based on the failure of the other parent to comply with the provisions of the order.

In all cases, the court will determine the best interests of the child in deciding whether to modify the terms of a custody order.

34

Child Support

"Every person has the duty to provide all reasonable support for that person's natural and adopted minor, unemancipated children..." — Arizona law

A parent generally must provide a child with a place to live, clothing, an education, attention, and medical care. In the case of divorce or legal separation, one parent typically will be required to pay child support to the other. This chapter discusses the obligation to pay child support. Information on calculating child support and obtaining legal forms is included at the end of the chapter.

Child Support Factors

By statute, child support must be the amount "reasonable and necessary for the support of a child, without regard to marital misconduct." The Arizona Supreme Court has established guidelines for determining the amount of child support, based on the following factors:

- The financial resources and needs of the child.
- The financial resources and needs of the custodial parent.
- The standard of living the child would have enjoyed had the marriage not been dissolved.
- The physical and emotional condition of the child, and the child's educational needs.

- The financial resources and needs of the noncustodial parent.
- The medical support plan for the child.
- Excessive or abnormal expenditures, destruction, concealment or fraudulent disposition of community, joint tenancy, and other property held in common.
- The duration of parenting time and related expenses.

The child support guidelines do not, however, replace the court's exercise of its discretion in determining the amount to be awarded. The court may deviate from the guidelines in appropriate cases.

The court will presume, in the absence of contrary testimony, that a noncustodial parent is capable of full-time employment at least at the federal adult minimum wage. This presumption does not apply to noncustodial parents who are under the age of 18 and who are attending high school. In awarding child support, the court generally will not attribute income to a parent greater than what would have been earned from full-time employment. Each parent should have the choice of working additional hours through overtime or at a second job without increasing the child support award.

Duration of Support

Child support continues until the child attains the age of majority (18 years). If, however, the child is attending high school when he or she attains the age of majority, support continues for so long as the child is actually attending high school, but then only until the child attains the age of 19 years. In the case of a mentally or physically disabled child, the court may order support to continue past age 18, and to be paid to the custodial parent, guardian, or child.

Medical Insurance

An order for child support will assign responsibility for providing medical insurance for the child, and will assign responsibility for the payment of his medical costs that are not covered by insurance. If the child is covered under an insurance plan provided by one parent's employer, the court will order that parent to provide medical insurance for the child, for so long as such coverage is offered through his employment.

Order of Assignment

In every child support case, the court will issue an order of assignment. The order of assignment will be directed to the employer of the parent who has been ordered to pay child support. It will require the employer to withhold from that parent's salary or wages the child support amount, and to transmit that amount directly to the support payment clearinghouse, for disbursement to the parent who is entitled to receive the support payment, unless the parties agree otherwise.

Exchange of Information

The court will order the parents to exchange financial information, such as tax returns, financial affidavits, and earnings statements, *every 24 months*. Unless the court orders otherwise, the parents must also exchange their addresses and the names and addresses of their employers when they exchange financial information.

Enforcement

Child support orders may be enforced through the contempt powers of the court. In addition, there are criminal and civil sanctions available to assist in the enforcement of a valid child support order. In the event of non-payment, the court may order that the non-paying parent be put in jail for willfully violating the child support order.

Modification

A party seeking to modify the amount of child support must prove that there has been a "substantial and continuing change of circumstances" since the entry of the child support order. A permanent disability or a big job promotion would likely qualify as a substantial and continuing change of circumstances, justifying a change in the amount of child support. If the modified amount of child support varies more than 15% from the existing amount, then that variation is good evidence of a substantial and continuing change of circumstances.

Child Support Calculator and Forms

To obtain an estimate of the amount of child support that will be payable in a given case, the reader can go to www. azcourts.gov/familylaw/childsupportcalculator.aspx. This Web site is maintained by the Arizona Supreme Court, and features an interactive PDF document that will calculate a child support amount based on the Arizona Child Support Guidelines. A copy of the Arizona Child Support Guidelines may also be obtained from the Supreme Court's Web site.

An excellent online resource for preparing family court documents and obtaining legal forms is maintained by the Maricopa County Superior Court, at www.ecourt.maricopa. gov/index.asp. This Web site contains interactive interviews that will assist the user in completing the forms necessary to create court documents for legal separation, dissolution, conciliation, and other family law matters. Once completed, the forms can be printed and then taken to the court for filing. Several other counties in Arizona also provide excellent online family law resources.

The child support calculator and the legal forms available on these Web sites are free to the public.

35

Spousal Maintenance (Alimony)

*Spousal maintenance is awardable to either spouse,
without regard to marital misconduct.*

In a proceeding for dissolution of marriage or legal separation,
the court may grant spousal maintenance (alimony) to either
spouse. Contrary to popular belief, 1) spousal maintenance
is not based on infidelity or marital misconduct, 2) it may be
granted to either a husband or wife, and 3) it is not awarded
with great frequency.

The court may grant spousal maintenance if it finds that the
spouse seeking maintenance:

- Lacks sufficient property, including property apportioned to the spouse, to provide for that spouse's
  reasonable needs; or
- Is unable to be self-sufficient through appropriate
  employment or is the custodian of a child whose age
  or condition is such that the custodian should not be
  required to seek employment outside the home or
  lacks earning ability in the labor market adequate to
  be self-sufficient; or
- Contributed to the educational opportunities of the
  other spouse; or
- Had a marriage of long duration and is of an age
  that may preclude the possibility of gaining employment adequate to be self-sufficient.

Arizona law provides that a spousal maintenance order, "shall be in an amount and for a period of time as the court deems just," without regard to marital misconduct. In determining the amount and duration of spousal maintenance, the court must consider the following 13 separate factors (these are from the statute):

- The standard of living established during the marriage;
- The duration of the marriage;
- The age, employment history, earning ability and physical and emotional condition of the spouse seeking maintenance;
- The ability of the spouse from whom maintenance is sought to meet that spouse's needs while meeting those of the spouse seeking maintenance;
- The comparative financial resources of the spouses, including their comparative earning abilities in the labor market;
- The contribution of the spouse seeking maintenance to the earning ability of the other spouse;
- The extent to which the spouse seeking maintenance has reduced that spouse's income or career opportunities for the benefit of the other spouse;
- The ability of both parties after the dissolution to contribute to the future educational costs of their mutual children;
- The financial resources of the party seeking maintenance, including marital property apportioned to that spouse, and that spouse's ability to meet his or her own needs independently;
- The time necessary to acquire sufficient education or training to enable the party seeking maintenance to find appropriate employment and whether such education or training is readily available;
- Excessive or abnormal expenditures, destruction, concealment or fraudulent disposition of community, joint tenancy, and other property held in common;

- The cost for the spouse who is seeking maintenance to obtain health insurance and the reduction in the cost of health insurance for the other spouse if the other spouse is able to convert family health insurance to employee health insurance after the marriage is dissolved; and
- All actual damages and judgments from conduct resulting in conviction of either spouse in which the other spouse or child was the victim.

Unlike an award of child support, for which the Arizona Supreme Court has established guidelines for determining the amount, there are no guidelines for determining the amount of spousal maintenance. The court has broad discretion to determine whether a party is entitled to spousal maintenance and, if so, the amount and duration of the spousal maintenance to which that party is entitled. In determining whether to award spousal maintenance or the amount of any such award, the court will not consider any veterans disability benefits awarded to the other spouse. The court's decision to grant or deny spousal maintenance usually will not be disturbed on appeal.

While statistics are hard to come by, anecdotal evidence suggests that spousal maintenance is awarded in less than 10% of all domestic relations cases in the state of Arizona. The frequency of spousal maintenance awards has declined in recent years as more couples both work outside the home and there are fewer marriages of long duration.

A person who is obligated to pay spousal maintenance pursuant to a court order and who willfully and without lawful excuse fails to comply with the order is guilty of a class 1 misdemeanor.

In a case in which spousal maintenance is awarded to a party, both the amount and duration of the award may subsequently be modified by the court. To modify a spousal maintenance award, a party must file a petition with the court, and prove a "substantial and continuing change of circumstances" since the original award. A spousal maintenance award will be modified based on the changed circumstances of the parties.

The parties in every case are free to agree that neither the amount nor the duration of the spousal maintenance may be modified, in which case the award will be non-modifiable.

Spousal maintenance is terminated by the death of the person paying it, or upon the death or remarriage of the person receiving it. Cohabitation with a member of the opposite sex by the person receiving spousal maintenance does not automatically trigger termination of the award.

The party paying spousal maintenance generally gets to deduct the amount paid on his or her income tax return, and conversely, the party receiving spousal maintenance must report the payments as income. The Internal Revenue Service has adopted rules to determine whether a payment from one former spouse to another will be treated as alimony for income tax purposes. Merely calling a payment spousal maintenance does not necessarily make it so for tax purposes. Child support payments, by comparison, are neither deducted by the payor nor reported as income by the recipient.

For summaries of actual cases in which spousal maintenance was awarded, the reader is invited to visit the author's Web site, www.loosebrown.com.

36

Orders of Protection

Protection against domestic violence

An order of protection may be issued by a court to prevent a person from committing an act of domestic violence. To obtain an order of protection, a person must file a verified petition with a magistrate, justice of the peace, or superior court judge. Any court in Arizona may issue or enforce an order of protection. If an action for dissolution of marriage, legal separation, or annulment is pending between the parties, the petition for order of protection should be filed in the Family Court.

The petition must contain certain information about the party who is filing it (the plaintiff), as well as the party against whom the order is sought (the defendant). It must also include a specific statement, including dates, of the domestic violence alleged.

A court will issue an order of protection if it determines that there is reasonable cause to believe that the defendant may commit an act of domestic violence or that he has committed an act of domestic violence within the past year (or within a longer period if good cause exists to consider a longer period). If the court denies the plaintiff's request, it may schedule a further hearing within 10 days, with notice to the defendant.

If a court issues an order of protection, it may: 1) prohibit the defendant from committing domestic violence; 2) grant one party the use and exclusive possession of the parties' residence;

3) prevent the defendant from contacting the plaintiff (or other designated persons) and from coming near the residence, place of employment or school of the plaintiff, or other designated locations or persons; 4) prohibit the defendant from possessing or purchasing a firearm, and require the surrender of existing firearms to local law enforcement; 5) require the defendant to complete a domestic violence offender treatment program; 6) grant other relief that is necessary to protect the victim; and/or 7) grant the plaintiff the exclusive care, custody and control of any animal owned by the parties, and order the defendant to stay away from the animal.

A party against whom an order of protection has been entered is entitled to one hearing on written request. The hearing will generally be held within 10 days from the date requested. If exclusive use of the home is awarded to the plaintiff, the hearing must be held within five days from the date requested. After the hearing, the court may change, terminate or continue the order of protection in effect.

Emergency orders of protection are available 24 hours a day throughout the state of Arizona. Superior court judges and commissioners, justices of the peace, and municipal court judges are immediately available to law enforcement officers through the use of cell phones and beepers. An emergency order will be issued whenever someone's safety is endangered, regardless of the time of day or night. An emergency order of protection expires at the close of the next business day after issuance, unless otherwise continued by the court.

An order of protection is an official court order. A person who disobeys the order may be arrested and prosecuted for the crime of interfering with judicial proceedings, as well as any other crime which he may have committed in disobeying the order.

A copy of the petition and the order of protection must be served on the defendant within one year from the date the order is signed. If the order is not served within one year, it expires. An order of protection is effective on the defendant the moment it is served on him. It expires one year from the date of service. On request of the plaintiff, the court will forward the order of protection to the proper law enforcement agency for service on the defendant. A fee is not charged for filing the petition, or for service of process.

37

Grandparents' Visitation Rights

Grandparents have visitation rights too.

Under the Arizona grandparent visitation statute, grandparents may be granted visitation rights if the court finds that it would be in the child's best interests and one of the following conditions exists: 1) the child's parents' marriage has been dissolved for at least three months; 2) a parent of the child has been deceased or missing for at least three months; or 3) the child was born out of wedlock.[5]

In determining the child's best interests, the court will consider all relevant factors, including the historical relationship between the child and the grandparent; the motivation of the party seeking visitation and the motivation of the party denying visitation; the amount of visitation time requested and the impact that visitation will have on the child's customary activities; and, if one or both of the child's parents are dead, the benefit in maintaining an extended family relationship.

If logistically possible and appropriate, the court will order visitation by a grandparent to occur when the child is residing or spending time with the parent through whom the grandparent claims a right of access to the child. A grandparent seeking to obtain visitation rights must petition for those rights in the same action in which the parents had their marriage dissolved. If no action for dissolution has been filed or if the court entering the decree of dissolution no longer has jurisdiction, a separate action must be filed by the grandparent in the county in which the child resides.

All visitation rights granted to a grandparent automatically terminate if the child has been adopted or placed for adoption. Thus, visitation rights granted to a grandparent will automatically terminate if the custodial parent's new spouse adopts the child.

38

Paternity Actions

"The issue…shall be whether or not the defendant is the father of the child." —Arizona paternity statute

Either parent, the child, or the state may file an action to establish paternity. Given the importance of establishing paternity, paternity proceedings have priority over other civil proceedings. When paternity is established, the court may award custody and parenting time, and will provide for the payment of child support. This chapter looks at paternity proceedings in Arizona.

Starting the Proceedings

Proceedings to establish paternity may be started during the mother's pregnancy or after the birth of the child. Paternity proceedings are started by the filing of a verified petition with the clerk of the superior court. The petition must allege that "a woman is delivered of a child" born out of wedlock or is pregnant with a child conceived out of wedlock, and that the defendant is the father of the child.

The alleged father must appear and answer the paternity petition within 20 days if he is served in Arizona, or within 30 days if he is served outside Arizona. The case will be set for trial within 60 days from the father's denial of paternity. In an action started before the birth of the child, a delay will be granted until the birth of the child for purposes of paternity tests.

If the alleged father fails to appear or otherwise answer the paternity petition, fails to take a court-ordered blood or genetic test, or voluntarily admits paternity, the court will enter an order of paternity. In other cases, paternity will be established by trial to the judge. (A party in a paternity action does *not* have a right of trial by jury.)

Genetic Testing

The court can order the mother, her child, and the alleged father to submit to genetic testing, and will direct that inherited characteristics to determine parentage, including blood and tissue type, be determined by testing procedures. An expert in the field of genetic markers will be agreed on by the parties or appointed by the court to analyze and interpret the results and report to the court.

If the results of the genetic tests indicate that the likelihood of the alleged father's paternity is 95% or greater, then he is presumed to be the father of the child. If the results of the examiner's report are challenged, the court may order an additional test to be made at the expense of the party requesting additional testing. The court will also determine the amount of the initial test costs to be paid by each party.

Presumption of Paternity

A man is presumed to be the father of a child if: 1) he and the mother were married at any time in the 10 months immediately before the birth, or the child is born within 10 months after the marriage is terminated; 2) genetic testing affirms at least a 95% probability of paternity; 3) a birth certificate is signed by the mother and father; or 4) a notarized or witnessed statement is signed by both parents acknowledging paternity.

Voluntary Acknowledgement of Paternity

The parent of a child born out of wedlock may establish paternity of a child by filing a document with the clerk of the superior court, the Department of Economic Security, or the Department of Health Services. The document may be 1) a notarized or witnessed statement that contains the social security numbers of both parents and is signed by both parents acknowledging paternity (if the acknowledgment is filed with the court, the filing party must remove the social security numbers and file them separately on a confidential data sheet), or 2) an agreement by the parents to be bound by the results of genetic testing, together with an affidavit from a certified laboratory that the tested father has not been excluded. On the filing of one of these documents, the clerk of the superior court will issue an order establishing paternity.

Paternity Order

If the father admits parentage or if the court determines that the male is the father, the court will direct the father to pay for the past support of the child, current support, and may direct the father to pay the costs of litigation. The court will not order past support retroactive to more than three years before the filing of the paternity suit, unless it finds good cause to do so.

The court will also direct the amount that the father must pay for the actual costs of the pregnancy, childbirth, any genetic testing, and other related costs. In ordering the payment of child support, the court will apply the child support guidelines. (For a discussion concerning the child support guidelines, please refer to Chapter 34.)

Child Custody

When paternity is established, the court may award custody and parenting time. The parent with whom the child has resided for the greater part of the last six months will have legal custody, unless otherwise ordered by the court.

39

Termination of Parent-Child Relationship

A parent's rights may be terminated for child neglect or abandonment.

A parent who abandons, neglects or abuses his child (under age 18) may lose his parental rights. Arizona law sets forth the grounds and the procedure for termination of the parent-child relationship.

Filing a Petition

A petition to terminate the parent-child relationship may be filed with the juvenile division of the superior court by any person who has a legitimate interest in the welfare of the child (under age 18). This would include a relative, a foster parent, a physician, the Department of Economic Security, or a private licensed child welfare agency.

After the petition has been filed, the clerk of the superior court will set a time and place for an initial hearing. Notice of the initial hearing and a copy of the petition must be given to the parents of the child, as well as to the child's guardian, the person having legal custody of the child, and any person standing in the position of parent to the child. There are other notice requirements for a Native American child. A potential father who fails to file a paternity action within 30 days after receiving legal notice that an adoption proceeding has been commenced, waives his right to notification regarding termination of parental rights and his consent is not required.

If a parent who has received proper notice does not appear at the initial hearing, the court may terminate the parent-child relationship as to that parent. At the initial hearing, the court will schedule a pretrial conference, schedule the termination hearing, and instruct the parents that failure to appear for any scheduled conference or hearing may result in automatic termination of that parent's rights.

Social Study

When a petition to terminate a parent-child relationship is filed, the court will usually order that a complete social study be conducted. The social study will include the circumstances of the petition, the social history, the present condition of the child and parent, proposed plans for the child, and any other facts pertinent to the parent-child relationship. The social study must include a recommendation as to whether or not the parent-child relationship should be terminated. The requirement of a social study may be waived if to do so would be in the best interests of the child.

Grounds for Termination

In a contested case, the court will determine at the termination hearing whether grounds exist to terminate the parent-child relationship. The court will consider the social study report, as well as other evidence, in making this determination. In evaluating the evidence, the court will consider the best interests of the child.

The parent-child relationship may be terminated if the court finds that the parent has abandoned the child. "Abandonment" means the failure of a parent to provide reasonable support and to maintain regular contact with the child, including providing normal supervision. The court must find that a parent has made only minimal efforts to support and communicate with the child. Failure to maintain a normal relationship with the child without good cause for a period of six months constitutes *prima facie* evidence of abandonment.

A parent's rights may also be terminated if the parent has neglected or wilfully abused a child. This abuse includes serious physical or emotional injury, or situations in which the parent knew (or should have known) that a person was abusing or neglecting a child.

It is also reason for termination that the parent is unable to discharge his parental responsibilities because of mental illness or chronic drug or alcohol abuse, and there are reasonable grounds to believe that the condition will continue for an indefinite period of time.

Other grounds for termination include a parent's conviction of a serious felony or prison sentence for a period of years; a father's failure to pursue paternity; a parent's relinquishment of rights or consent to adoption; prolonged or repeated out-of-home placements; unknown identity of the parent; and another termination within two years, coupled with that parent's inability to discharge parental responsibilities for the same reason. In considering grounds for termination, the court will take into account any substantiated allegations of abuse or neglect committed in another state.

Termination Order

If the court terminates the parent-child relationship, it will appoint a guardian for the child and make an order fixing responsibility for the child's support. The parent-child relationship may be terminated with respect to one parent without affecting the relationship between the child and the other parent.

An order terminating the parent-child relationship divests the parent and the child of all rights, privileges and duties with respect to each other, except the right of the child to inherit and receive support from the parent. The right of inheritance and support can only be terminated by an order of adoption. Until then, the child retains the right of inheritance from the parents, and the parents remain individually responsible for the support of the child.

All files, records, reports and other papers relating to a termination proceeding are withheld from public inspection.

40

Adoption

Consent to adoption cannot be given until 72 hours
after the birth of the child.

When an adoption order is entered, the relationship of parent and child is established between the adoptive parent and the adopted child. The child has all of the legal rights and privileges as though he were born to the adoptive parent in lawful wedlock. Conversely, the parental relationship between the natural parents and the adopted child is completely severed (unless the adoption is by the child's stepparent).

An adoption may be either an "agency placement adoption" or a "direct placement adoption." An agency placement adoption is a proceeding in which an adoption agency has been authorized to place the child for adoption. A direct placement adoption is a proceeding in which a particular person has been authorized to adopt the child. The authorization is given by the child's parents after the child is born.

Any child in Arizona under the age of 18 years may be adopted. A husband and wife may jointly adopt a child.

Preadoption Certification

Before a person may petition to adopt a child, that person must be certified by the court as acceptable to adopt children. A certificate will be issued only after an investigation is conducted by an officer of the court, by a licensed agency, or by the

Department of Economic Security (DES). The investigation will include the prospective adoptive parent's social history, financial condition, moral fitness, religious background, physical and mental health, and other facts bearing on the issue of fitness.

The person or agency conducting the investigation will submit a written report to the court, which will include a recommendation for certifying the applicant as being acceptable or unacceptable. The court will certify the applicant as being acceptable or nonacceptable to adopt based on the report. A certification remains valid for 18 months, but may be extended for additional one-year periods if there are no material changes in circumstances.

The requirement for preadoption certification does not apply if the prospective adoptive parent is the spouse of the birth or legal parent of the child, or is an uncle, aunt, adult sibling, grandparent or great-grandparent of the child, and in other limited circumstances.

A person who is not certified as acceptable but who has custody of a child, except for a stepparent, close family relative or guardian of the child, must petition the court for an order permitting that person to keep custody of the child pending certification. The person must file the petition not later than five days after he obtains custody of the child.

Consent to Adoption

Generally, a court will not grant an adoption unless consent to adopt is obtained from the child's mother, the child's father, the child (if 12 years of age or older), any court-appointed guardian with authority to consent to adoption, and, in the case of an agency placement adoption, the agency. Consent must be obtained from DES if it has been given consent to place the child for adoption by a parent whose consent would otherwise be necessary, or if it otherwise has legal authority to place the child for adoption, although the court may waive the requirement for consent if to do so is clearly in the child's best interest. It is not necessary to obtain consent from a parent whose parental rights have been terminated, or from a potential father who fails to file a paternity action within 30 days after receiving legal notice that the adoption is planned.

All consents to adoption, except from the child, must be in writing and signed by the person giving the consent, be witnessed by two credible adults, and be acknowledged by the person giving consent before a notary public. *A consent that is given before 72 hours after the birth of the child is invalid.* A consent to adopt is irrevocable, unless it was obtained by fraud, duress, or undue influence. Except for payment of certain expenses, a person may not be compensated for giving or obtaining consent to place a child for adoption. (In any event, a person cannot pay the living expenses of a birth parent that exceed $1,000 without permission of the court.)

When a consent to adoption is given, the birth parent will usually also give a notarized statement granting or withholding permission for the child, when he reaches 18 years of age, to obtain information about himself and the birth parent. The decision to grant or withhold information may be changed by the birth parent at any time by the filing of a notarized statement with the court.

Before placing a child for adoption, DES, the licensed agency, or the person placing the child is required to compile and provide to the prospective adoptive parent detailed written nonidentifying information, including a health and genetic history, and all nonidentifying information about the birth parents or members of their families.

Petition to Adopt

A petition to adopt can be filed in the juvenile division of the superior court in the county in which the child resides. The petition must state the name of the prospective adoptive parent, but the child to be adopted may be referred to by a fictitious name. If a change of name for the child is desired, the new name should be stated in the petition.

Adoption Hearing; Social Study

After a petition to adopt has been filed, the court clerk will set a time and place for the hearing. All persons interested in the adoption must be given notice of the hearing. DES, a licensed agency, or an officer of the court will conduct a social study before the hearing date. The social study will include all information that is pertinent to the adoption proceedings, and it will contain a recommendation for or against the proposed adoption. The social study must be submitted to the court at least 10 days before the adoption hearing.

Not less than 10 days before the adoption hearing, the prospective adoptive parent must file with the court a verified accounting of all fees, payments, disbursements, or commitments made by him in connection with the adoption. The birth mother must sign an affidavit that verifies that she has been given written notice and understands that the payment of her living expenses by another person does not obligate her to place the child for adoption. These requirements do not apply if an agency is involved in the adoption, or if a stepparent is the prospective adoptive parent.

The adoption hearing will be conducted in an informal manner. The prospective adoptive parent, his spouse, and the child to be adopted must attend. The matters discussed at the hearing will not be disclosed to any person who is not present. If all of the adoption requirements have been met and the court believes the adoption is in the best interests of the child, the court will order the adoption. The order may change the name of the child to that of the adoptive parent. The court will send an order to the department of vital records to change the child's name on the child's birth certificate, and to add the name of the adoptive parent thereto.

Communications Agreements

The parties to an adoption may enter into an agreement regarding communications with the child. Under this agreement, the adoptive parent may terminate contact between the birth parent and the adoptive child at any time. The court will approve the agreement, unless it finds that communication between the parties is in the child's best interests.

All files, records, reports, and other papers in an adoption proceeding are withheld from public inspection.

41

Change of Name

"I don't like your Christian name. I'd like you to change it."
—Thomas Beecham, to his future wife

The name given to a person by his parents at birth is not necessarily the name that he has to keep for the rest of his life. The legal process to change a name in Arizona is relatively quick and easy. (This brings to mind an old Johnny Cash song, *"A Boy Named Sue,"* which humorously illustrates the importance of a name.)

If a person desires to change his name, he must file an application in the superior court in the county of his residence. In the application, he will set forth the reasons for the change of name and the name he wishes to adopt.

The parent or guardian of a minor (under age 18) may file an application for change of the name of the minor. The application will be filed in the county of the minor's residence.

A person who files an application for change of name must indicate, under penalty of perjury: 1) if he has been convicted of a felony; 2) if felony charges are pending against him for certain criminal offenses involving theft, forgery, fraud, perjury, or any other offense involving false statements; 3) if he is knowingly changing the person's name to that of another person for the purpose of committing any criminal offense previously enumerated; 4) he is making the application solely for the best interest of the person; and 5) he acknowledges that the change of name will not release the person from any prior obligations or harm any property rights or actions in the original name.

In some cases, the court may order that notice of the name change application be given by publication or by service upon any party interested in the proceeding. In the case of divorced parents, notice of an application to change the name of a minor must be given to the noncustodial parent, whose name the child may no longer have if the application is granted.

Upon the filing of the application, the court will set the case for a hearing. The person seeking a name change must attend the hearing and explain to the judge his reasons for wanting to change the name. The court may enter an order that the adopted name of the party be substituted for the original name. In the case of a minor, the court will consider the best interests of the child in determining whether to enter an order changing the name of the child. If the minor is 14 years of age or older, he must sign a notarized consent or attend the hearing.

In every case, the court will consider the criteria in the application in determining whether to grant a request for change of name. A crime victim or a prosecutor has the right to contest any legal name change at any time before entry of the order changing the name, or up to one year later.

The change of name does not release the person from any obligation which he incurred under his original name, nor does it affect any property rights that he acquired in his original name.

There are two other ways to change a person's name. First, in an adoption proceeding, the court will give the adopted child the name of his adoptive parents. The state registrar will then issue a new certificate of birth for the adopted child. Second, in the case of a divorce, annulment or legal separation, the domestic relations court may restore to the wife the use of her former name if she requests it. In those cases, the decree will contain a provision for the change of name.

42

Delegation of Parental Powers

"If anything can go wrong, it will" —Murphy's Law

In Arizona, a parent of a minor (under age 18) may delegate to another person any powers he may have regarding the care, custody, or property of the minor child, except the power to consent to marriage or adoption of the minor.

A parent desiring to delegate his parental powers pursuant to this law must execute a power of attorney. (For the legal requirements, please refer to Chapter 55 on durable powers of attorney.) A parent cannot delegate his parental powers by a power of attorney for longer than six months, but there is no limitation on the number of powers of attorney that he may execute. The six-month period may thus be extended by the execution of successive six-month powers of attorney.

Any parent leaving his child in the care of another for an extended period of time would do well to consider delegating some or all of his parental powers to the child's temporary caregiver. By so doing, a parent may be able to avoid the consequences of Murphy's Law.

43

Parents' Liability for Child's Misconduct

"Children have never been very good at listening to their elders, but they have never failed to imitate them." —James Baldwin

Any act of malicious or willful misconduct of a minor (under age 18) which results in injury to the person or property of another, including theft or shoplifting, is by law attributable to the parents or legal guardian having custody or control of the minor. It is not a defense that the parents or guardian could not have anticipated the minor's misconduct.

The parents or guardian having custody or control are jointly and separately liable with the minor for any damages resulting from the minor's malicious or willful misconduct, up to $10,000 per occurrence.

Nothing in the law limits the rights of an insurance company to exclude coverage for the acts of a minor imputed to his parents or legal guardian pursuant to this section. Accordingly, parents and guardians would do well to check their insurance policies to determine if coverage for this type of liability is provided.

PART FOUR

Wills and Estates

44

Wills

A will is a "legal declaration of a man's intention, which he wills to be performed after his death." — Quote from a 1939 case

No particular form of will is required, so long as there has been compliance with the legal requirements. The law of wills differs from state to state. This chapter is based entirely on Arizona law.

Any person 18 years or older and of "sound mind" may execute a will. A person who executes a will is called a "testator." The law does not require any residence or citizenship, so that nonresidents of Arizona and aliens may make valid wills in Arizona.

There are many ways that property may be disposed of after death: a) under a will or living trust; b) pursuant to joint tenancy and community property survivorship provisions; c) by "pay on death" clauses and insurance contract designations; and d) by informal lists (for tangible personal property, such as jewelry and furniture). The most common way for property to be disposed of after death is under a will, although living trusts are becoming more popular and, in many cases, have the important benefit of avoiding taxes and probate. (Living trusts and other forms of property disposition are discussed in subsequent chapters.)

Legal Requirements

A will must be signed by the testator or by someone at his direction and in his conscious presence. A person may sign by making a mark ("X") if illiterate or incapacitated. Two attesting witnesses must sign the will. Interestingly, there is no requirement that the witnesses sign in the presence of the testator or each other, although most often all three persons (the testator and two witnesses) sign the will at the same time in each other's presence.

Under Arizona law, a beneficiary under the will may act as a witness. The law in many other states is different. Earlier Arizona law invalidated the whole will if a beneficiary acted as a witness.

Foreign wills do not necessarily have to be redone in Arizona to be valid. A written will is valid if it is executed in compliance with the law of the state or country in which it is executed. Therefore, a will that was valid when it was executed outside the state of Arizona is valid in Arizona, regardless of where it was executed or whether it meets Arizona's requirements for execution.

A will may be made "self-proved" either at the time of the original execution or later. A self-proved will contains an acknowledgment by the testator and affidavit of the witnesses before a notary public. The advantage of a self-proved will is greatest in a will contest. If a self-proved will is contested in court, the formalities of proper execution are conclusively presumed.

Holographic and Oral Wills

A "holographic will" is a will that is in the testator's handwriting and not witnessed. Holographic wills are valid in Arizona if the signature and material provisions are in the handwriting of the testator. A testator can create a valid holographic will by using a preprinted form, as long as the form is signed and the designation of beneficiaries and the estate appointment are in the testator's own handwriting. A holographic will does not need to be dated.

Arizona formerly allowed oral wills if made in the testator's last illness before three witnesses, but that statute has been repealed. An oral will is no longer valid.

Separate Writing for Tangible Personal Property

The law allows a separate writing to dispose of items of *tangible personal property*. Tangible personal property is property which may be felt or touched, such as a chair, a computer, or a watch. The purpose of this provision is to allow a testator to prepare a separate list of things, like furniture, household goods, jewelry, antiques, pictures, guns, and other personal effects, that the testator wants distributed to relatives and friends. The list does not have to comply with the normal formalities for execution (discussed earlier), but it must be referred to in a properly executed will and must be in the handwriting of the testator and signed by him. The list can be made up after the execution of the will and changed from time to time if the testator so wishes. It is a particularly useful provision if the testator has not thought through his wishes with respect to these items at the time he executes his will, if his possessions are likely to change, or if he may want to change the list later.

Although there is no limit on the value of the tangible personal property that can be disposed of by such a list, it would be unwise to use the list as a means of passing valuable jewelry, antiques, collections, paintings, vehicles, or the like. These items should be specifically disposed of by the will, and the list used only for items of relatively small value. It should be noted that a testator may execute an attested will and later execute in his own handwriting a document disposing of any kind of property he wishes. In other words, a valid holographic will can revoke the provisions of the attested will, and the holographic will is not limited to tangible personal property.

Personal Representative

A testator may nominate a personal representative in his will. A personal representative (formerly known as an executor) administers the will following the testator's death. Any person 18 years of age or older is qualified to serve as a personal representative unless the court finds that person to be unsuitable.

A person who is incompetent would, for example, be unsuitable to serve as personal representative. A corporation or other legal entity may also serve as a personal representative. Neither Arizona residence nor United States citizenship is required for a personal representative. Of course, consent of the person or institution to be named should be secured prior to completing the will to assure that the nominee will serve.

The testator may request that the personal representative serve without bond. A bond is a form of security that in most cases takes the form of an insurance policy. It protects the beneficiaries in case the personal representative fails to properly perform his duties. In the absence of a waiver of bond in the will, the court may require a bond. Qualified trust companies and banks are not required to post bonds, however.

Once appointed by the court, the powers of the personal representative are very broad and comprehensive. Generally, no further court authorization or approval is required for the personal representative to exercise those powers.

A personal representative is entitled to reasonable compensation for his services, and the will may specify the amount of the fee.

Guardian for Minor Children

A testator can also nominate a guardian for minor children in a validly executed will. (For a discussion regarding guardians, please refer to Chapter 58.) A guardian is a person who is responsible generally for the health, welfare and safety of a minor. It is good practice for the parent of a minor child to nominate a guardian for the child in the event the other parent predeceases the testator, or is not able to care for the child after the testator's death. It should be noted, however, that a minor 14 years of age or over may object to the appointment of the guardian nominated in the will.

Revocation

Two distinguishing characteristics of a will are that it is cancelable (revocable) prior to death, and that it takes effect only at death. A testator may cancel a will in whole or in part by executing a subsequent will that revokes the previous will or part expressly or by inconsistency, or by performing a "revocatory act." Burning, tearing, canceling, obliterating, or destroying the will or any part of it with the intent to revoke it will be sufficient. The physical act must be accompanied by the present intent to revoke. The requisite physical act can even be performed by a third person if directed by the testator to be done in his presence.

A will may also be revoked by operation of law. A divorce or annulment revokes the provisions in a will in favor of the ex-spouse and his or her relatives. In cases where there is a felonious and intentional killing of the testator, the provisions of a will benefiting the killer will be revoked.

If a testator marries after executing his will and does not provide for his spouse, the surviving spouse is entitled to a share equal to the share she would have received had the decedent died without a will. This is another situation in which a will is changed by operation of law, and not by any act of the testator.

Benefits of Having a Will

Irrespective of the primary means by which assets are disposed of at the time of death (*e.g.*, will, living trust, joint tenancy, etc.), a validly executed will has a place in almost every estate plan. If the will is the instrument by which all or part of the assets will be disposed of, then its importance is primary in the estate plan. However, even in a case where a living trust or some other will-substitute is used to dispose of property, a will is still valuable to enable the testator to use a separate writing for tangible personal property, to give funeral and burial directions, and to nominate a guardian for minor children. In cases where a living trust has been prepared, a will ensures that any assets outside the trust at the testator's death are poured over to the trust.

Ten Common Misconceptions About Wills

1. **If I don't have a will, my property will go to the state.** False. If you don't have a will, your property will go to your heirs under the law of descent and distribution in Arizona. Your property will go to the state only if you die without a will *and* you have no living relative to inherit it.

2. **If I have a will, all of my property will automatically pass under it.** False. Some or all of your property may pass outside your will by reason of survivorship provisions, joint title, pay-on-death clauses, and beneficiary designations in deeds and contracts. For instance, life insurance proceeds will be payable to the beneficiaries that you have designated in the insurance contract, regardless of the terms of your will.

3. **The will that I executed before I moved to Arizona is invalid.** False. If your will was valid in the state or country in which it was executed, it is valid in Arizona. (This does not mean, however, that it may not be a good idea to update your will in Arizona.)

4. **I have to execute a living trust to avoid taxes on my estate.** False. Most estates will *not* be subject to taxation with or without a living trust. So long as the value of the decedent's estate does not exceed the applicable estate tax exclusion, there will be no federal estate tax owed. *See* Unified Credit Exemption Amounts in Appendix B. If you are married, you can leave an unlimited amount to your spouse without payment of any estate taxes.

5. **If I execute a will, my estate will be subjected to costly attorney fees and probate charges when I die.** False. It is not inherently expensive to probate a will in Arizona. An informal and inexpensive probate process is available in most cases. There are no

separate probate fees, other than a small filing fee to start the case.

6. **It is always less expensive to leave my property under a living trust than a will.** False. In some cases, it is actually more expensive to create a living trust than to informally probate an estate. It depends on the nature and value of your assets. (Please refer to the next chapter for a discussion concerning living trusts.)

7. **If I execute a will, I will be unable to create a trust for my children.** False. One or more trusts can be created in a will. These are known as "testamentary trusts," and take effect upon the death of the person executing the will (the "testator"). By use of a testamentary trust, you can set aside money or property for the future benefit of your children. The testamentary trust will be administered by the trustee you appoint in your will.

8. **If my estate is probated under a will, my assets will be tied up for years in the courts.** False. Informal probate can be started almost immediately after your death, allows the personal representative immediate access to your assets, and in most cases, can be completed in nine months or less.

9. **My will must be filed after it is executed.** False. There is no provision for the filing of a will in Arizona, until after the death of the testator. The original stays with the testator after execution.

10. **It is better to keep my will in a safe deposit box than at home.** False. Access to a safe deposit box is often difficult and time consuming after the death of the person renting the box. A better place to keep your will is at home with your other important papers, where family members can easily access it.

45

Living Trusts

*A trust may be used to avoid probate and
eliminate or reduce estate taxes.*

Any discussion about living trusts should properly start with a definition of the term. A living trust is a legal entity that is created and holds title to assets during the life of the person who places assets inside the trust. That person is known as the *settlor*.

The trust is created by executing a trust agreement, and transferring the settlor's assets to the trust. The trust holds title to the assets. However, even though the settlor relinquishes *title* to the assets, the settlor still retains *control* of those assets. A trustee appointed by the settlor manages the trust assets. In most cases, the settlor is also the initial trustee. As the trustee of the trust, the settlor continues to have the same power to buy, sell, transfer, and otherwise control the trust assets.

Illustration #1: John executes a trust agreement, thereby creating a living trust. John then transfers title to his house to himself, *as the trustee of his trust*. John is both the settlor and the initial trustee in this example. Although the trust now holds title to John's house, John still retains control of it.

The trust is *revocable*, which means that it can be modified or terminated by the settlor for so long as the settlor is alive and competent to make a contract. In some sophisticated estate plans, it may be desirable to create one or more *irrevoca-*

ble trusts, but irrevocable trusts are beyond the scope of this chapter.

Parties to a Trust

As we saw in Illustration #1 above, a person who creates a revocable trust may serve dual functions simultaneously. The settlor is the person who creates the trust. (The Internal Revenue Service refers to the settlor as the grantor, and to the trust as a grantor's trust.)

The *trustee* is the person who handles the administration of the trust. When a trust is first created, the trustee is usually the same person as the settlor. When a married couple creates a trust, both spouses usually serve as the co-trustees.

The *surviving trustee* is the person who continues to manage the trust after one of the original trustees has died. The surviving spouse is typically the primary *beneficiary* as well as the surviving trustee. A *successor trustee* is a person or entity that is named to succeed the surviving trustee upon death or incompetence. The successor trustee has the same powers as the original trustees.

Assets

For a trust to be effective in avoiding probate and minimizing taxation, all of the settlor's assets should be placed inside the trust. Assets may include bank accounts, real estate, and motor vehicles. The process involves simply changing the title to the assets to the trust. The person who controls the assets does not change, only the title to the assets does.

Except for real estate deeds, transferring assets into the trust should have no cost. The settlor is the person who (with the assistance of counsel where necessary) places the assets into the trust, and is the same person who has the right to also transfer those assets from the trust. Assets acquired after the trust is created should also be titled in the name of the trust.

Illustration #2: John sells his house after it has been transferred into the trust, and he buys another. The new house should also be titled in the name of the trust.

Because the settlor owns nothing in his name (all of the assets were placed in the trust), there is nothing to probate upon his death. If the settlor is married, the surviving spouse typically becomes the surviving trustee and, as such, continues to have the same power to buy, sell, or transfer the assets. Upon the death of the surviving spouse, the same situation applies as before. Since no assets were in the name of the deceased, there is nothing to probate. The trust document will identify who is to act as the successor trustee upon the death of the surviving spouse.

Types of Trusts

The trust document can take one of several basic forms. The two most basic forms, however, are the A Trust and the A-B Trust. There are other forms of trusts (such as the A-B-C Trust), but they are best left to be explained by estate planning counsel retained for that purpose.

One important reason for having a trust is to avoid paying unnecessary estate taxes. The form that best suits a particular situation will depend on the person's marital status, the value of the estate, the applicable estate tax exclusion (see Appendix B), and the potential distribution desired for the heirs.

The A Trust can be used for single persons or married couples, but must always be used when only one person is involved. The A-B Trust is generally used when two people are involved in the trust, whether they are married or unmarried. Married couples whose combined estate exceeds the applicable exclusion amount should consider the A-B Trust in order to take full advantage of the unified credit exclusion. Upon the death of one spouse, half of the assets will flow down into the B (or decedent's) Trust, and the other half of the assets will flow down to the survivor in the A (or survivor's) Trust. The entire estate will remain available to be used by the survivor, subject to certain restrictions imposed by the IRS.

Illustration #3: John and Mary, a married couple, create an A-B Trust. Their combined estate is worth $2,000,000 and the applicable exclusion, for discussion purposes, is $1,000,000.

Assuming John dies, half of the assets, worth $1,000,000, will flow down into the B (or decedent's) Trust, and the other half of the assets, also worth $1,000,000, will flow down to Mary in the A (or survivor's) Trust. The entire estate will remain available to be used by Mary, subject to the restrictions discussed in the following paragraph. There will be no estate tax owed as a result of John's death, and if the value of the assets in the survivor's trust continues to not exceed the exclusion amount, there will be no estate tax owed on Mary's death.

In most revocable trusts, the surviving spouse is named as the beneficiary of the B Trust (as in the above illustration) and, accordingly, has the right to all of the income of the B Trust, the right to use the principal in the B Trust for certain enumerated purposes, and the right to spend, each year, $5,000 or 5% of the assets, whichever is greater, in the B Trust, for any reason. The surviving spouse retains absolute control over the assets in the A Trust.

The use of a revocable trust in an estate plan can avoid probate and eliminate or reduce estate tax in some cases. For this reason, every person owning assets should consider a living trust.

46

Special-Purpose Trusts

A special trust may further specific estate planning goals.

A trust is a legal entity that is created and holds title to assets during the life of the person who places assets inside the trust. The use of a special trust may be desirable to meet the unique challenges presented by a blended-family situation (where the family structure has changed because of divorce, separation or remarriage), or to avoid payment of estate taxes. Here, we examine two common forms of special trusts.

- *Qualified Terminable Interest Property (QTIP) Trust.* The QTIP trust is often used when one spouse has remarried. It is a special trust that lets the maker of the trust, called the settlor, use the unlimited marriage deduction, provide for his spouse after his death, and defer potential estate taxes until the second death while retaining ultimate control over the distribution of his property. In using a QTIP trust, a certain portion of the settlor's assets is transferred upon death into a trust that pays income (and potentially principal) to the settlor's spouse for her lifetime. At the spouse's death, the principal passes to the beneficiaries that the settlor has designated.
- *Irrevocable Life Insurance Trust (ILIT).* The ILIT trust allows an insurance policy to be held in a trust so that it will not be included in the settlor's taxable

estate. In order for the settlor to receive full tax advantages offered by an ILIT, he cannot name himself or his spouse as the trustee. After January 1, 2009, an individual can contribute $13,000 annually ($26,000 per married couple) per beneficiary to pay the premiums on the life insurance policy held in the trust. Upon the death of the settlor, or the settlor and spouse, the life insurance policy's proceeds are paid to the trust. The trustee then distributes that money to the beneficiaries as outlined by the terms of the trust.

The use of any trust for estate planning purposes ultimately will depend on a variety of factors, including the size and complexity of the estate, the need to avoid taxes, and the settlor's desire to distribute assets outright or in trust. As shown above, the use of a special trust may help further the settlor's specific goals and objectives.

47

Informal Probate

"[T]he entire probate procedure can be accomplished without court supervision or involvement."

The term "probate" refers to the legal procedure for the administration of a deceased person's estate. In many cases, probate is a quick and efficient way to transfer the assets of a person who has died (the "decedent") to his heirs. (In other cases, the transfer of assets is best accomplished by the use of a trust or nonprobate transfers, which are discussed in other chapters of this book.) About 10,000 probate cases are filed each year in the state of Arizona.

The basic philosophy of the Arizona probate code is to minimize court involvement. It allows for the "informal" administration of most estates. This means that, in most cases, the entire probate procedure can be accomplished *without* court supervision or involvement. If an informal proceeding is not available or desired, the probate code provides for a "formal" proceeding. In a formal proceeding, the court is directly involved in the probate procedure.

Because informal probate proceedings are utilized in most cases, this chapter is devoted to the informal probate process in Arizona.

Opening the Estate

The first step in the administration of an estate is to have a person appointed to handle estate affairs. This person is known as the "personal representative" (formerly, this person was called the "executor"). To get a personal representative appointed, a person interested in the estate may file an application with the probate registrar (the registrar is a person authorized by law to make certain probate decisions, but he is not a judge). An application for informal probate cannot be filed sooner than five days, nor later than two years, after the decedent's death.

If there is a will, an estate will normally be opened by an application for both informal probate of the will *and* appointment of a personal representative. A person nominated in a will has priority for appointment as personal representative. If there is no will, the probate application will merely request the appointment of a particular person to be the personal representative.

The following persons have priority (in the order listed) for appointment as personal representative: 1) the person nominated in a will; 2) the surviving spouse who is also a beneficiary under the will; 3) other will beneficiaries; 4) the surviving spouse; 5) other heirs; 6) 45 days after the decedent's death, any creditor; and 7) the public fiduciary. Where several persons share priority, they must agree on which of them will be appointed as personal representative. If they are unable to agree, the court will appoint one or more of them in a formal proceeding.

Notice of Appointment

If a will is informally admitted to probate, the personal representative must give the heirs and each devisee (a devisee is a person designated in a will to receive estate assets) a written statement that the will has been admitted to probate by the court, and that an heir has four months to contest the probate. A copy of the will must be sent with the statement.

The personal representative must also send a statement to the heirs and devisees informing them of the appointment, the personal representative's name and address, whether or not a bond has been filed, and a description of the court where official papers regarding the estate are on file. This statement may be combined with the statement described in the preceding paragraph. The statement must be given within 10 days after the appointment of the personal representative.

Personal Representative's Duties

A personal representative is a fiduciary. This means that he has a duty of loyalty to the beneficiaries and creditors of the estate. The personal representative must be cautious and prudent in dealing with estate assets. The assets must never be used for the personal representative's benefit or mixed with other assets. A personal representative is prohibited by law from participating in any transaction that involves a conflict of interest.

The personal representative's first duty is to protect the estate property. This means that the personal representative must immediately find, identify, and take possession of the estate assets. If there is reason to believe that someone is concealing estate assets, the personal representative may file a lawsuit against the person who is hiding the assets. In that suit, the personal representative may examine the person regarding any property or papers relating to the decedent's estate.

The personal representative is required to prepare an inventory of the estate assets within 90 days after his appointment. The inventory must list all of the probate assets and their values as of the date of death. Once the inventory is prepared, the personal representative may file it with the court and mail a copy of it to the heirs and devisees, or may simply mail a copy of it to the heirs and devisees. If the family does not want the information in the inventory to be made part of the public record, the personal representative should not file it with the court.

Family Allowances

The personal representative has the power to set allowances for the maintenance of the family during the probate process. These statutory allowances, as they are called, include a homestead allowance, exempt property allowance, and family allowance. The surviving spouse and dependent children are generally eligible to receive these allowances, in the amounts set by statute.

Claims of Creditors

The personal representative must publish notice to creditors once a week for three successive weeks in a newspaper of general circulation in the county of appointment. The notice will announce the appointment of the personal representative and tell creditors of the estate that they must present their claims to the personal representative, at the address specified in the notice, within four months from the date of first publication. If a claim is not presented within the four-month creditors' claim period, it will not be paid. A notice must also be mailed by the personal representative to all persons whom he knows are creditors, or those who can be reasonably ascertained.

If a claim is disputed, the personal representative may disallow it, or negotiate a compromise with the person making it. The personal representative has a duty to investigate each claim and decide whether to allow it or disallow it. To disallow a claim, the personal representative must, within 60 days after the time for presentation has expired, file a notice of disallowance and notify the claimant accordingly. Failure by the personal representative to disallow the claim has the effect of allowing it.

The personal representative must pay all valid debts and expenses (including taxes) owed by the estate. If there are not enough assets to pay all of the charges against the estate, the personal representative must determine which debts and expenses should be paid according to law. The personal representative may be personally liable to the beneficiaries or to creditors with unpaid claims, if he pays a debt or expense that should not be paid.

Distribution of Assets

After payment of all debts and expenses, the personal representative must distribute the remaining assets as directed in the will. If there is no will, the assets must be distributed to the heirs as provided by law. The personal representative owes a duty of impartiality to all heirs and devisees under a will. This means that they must all be treated alike. Nonetheless, the personal representative, in some cases, may distribute the assets in cash or in kind, or partially in cash and partially in kind. For distributions in kind, the property must be valued at fair market value at the time of distribution. The personal representative may be personally liable if he makes an improper distribution of estate assets.

Personal Representative's Compensation

The personal representative is entitled to reasonable compensation for his services. Arizona law does not designate percentage fees for the personal representative's work or state how much he should be paid for his services. The personal representative should keep detailed records of all time expended by him on estate matters and receipts to prove out-of-pocket expenses. In determining whether a fee is reasonable, several factors will be considered, including the time required, the fee normally charged for similar services, the nature and value of estate assets, and the results obtained for the estate.

The personal representative must prepare a final account at the end of the administration process. The account must contain a full disclosure of the handling of the estate, including income received, expenses paid, and gains or losses on the sale of estate assets. The account must be sent to all persons who are affected by it.

The court does not supervise informal probates or the conduct of the personal representatives who administer them. However, if any person who has an interest in the estate believes that the estate has not been properly handled or that the fees charged by the attorney or personal representative are not reasonable under the circumstances, he may request that the court review the personal representative's accounting.

Closing the Estate

After distribution of the estate has been completed, the estate must be closed. To close an estate informally, the personal representative will file a verified statement (known as a "closing statement") that he has 1) published notice to creditors; 2) fully administered the estate (including settlement of claims, expenses and taxes, and distribution of the assets); 3) sent a copy to all distributees and to creditors with unpaid claims; and 4) furnished an account to all interested parties. The court will usually expect the estate to be completely administered and closed by no later than one year after the appointment of the personal representative.

The personal representative cannot be sued for breach of duties after six months from the filing of the closing statement, except for fraud, misrepresentation, or inadequate disclosure. The appointment of the personal representative terminates one year after the closing statement is filed, unless proceedings are pending.

48

Rules for Determining Heirs

Arizona's Law of Intestate Succession

The Arizona Probate Code provides rules for determining heirs. These rules apply in cases where the deceased person (the "decedent") fails to leave a will, or not all of the decedent's assets are disposed of by the will (or by one or more nonprobate transfers). In those cases, the Code determines the decedent's heirs, and the shares to which those heirs are entitled.

The rules are:

- If the decedent was survived by a spouse but no issue (children, grandchildren, or other descendants), then all assets to spouse.
- If the decedent was survived by a spouse and issue, all of whom are also issue of the surviving spouse, then all assets to spouse.
- If the decedent was survived by a spouse and issue, one or more of whom are not issue of the surviving spouse, then one-half of the decedent's separate property to spouse, and the decedent's half of community property and one-half of the decedent's separate property to issue.
- If the decedent was survived by issue but no spouse, then all assets to issue (by right of representation).[1]
- If the decedent was not survived by a spouse or issue, then all assets to surviving parents equally.

- If the decedent was not survived by a spouse, issue or parent, then all assets to brothers and sisters equally (issue of a deceased sibling, *i.e.*, nephews and nieces, take by representation).
- If the decedent was not survived by a spouse, issue, parent, sibling, or issue of a sibling, then one-half of assets to paternal grandparents equally (or their issue if both deceased), and one-half of assets to maternal grandparents equally (or their issue if both deceased).
- If the decedent was not survived by a grandparent or issue on one side of the family, then all assets to grandparents or their issue on the other side.
- If the decedent was not survived by issue of parents or grandparents, then all assets to state of Arizona.

Some other rules:
- The terms of a valid will supersede the above rules (*i.e.*, the terms of a will replace any rule).
- A person who does not survive the decedent by 120 hours is deemed not to have survived the decedent.
- Relatives of the half blood inherit the same share as if they were of the whole blood.
- A child in gestation is treated as living at that time if the child lives at least 120 hours after its birth.
- A person is the child of his natural parents, regardless of their marital status.
- An adopted person is the child of his adopting parents.

49

Small Estate Affidavits

How to avoid probate in small estates

It is possible to avoid probate entirely in small estates by the use of affidavits to collect the property and assets of the deceased person (the "decedent"). This chapter explains how to use small estate affidavits to avoid probate.

Hypothetical Case

Let us use a hypothetical case to explore the process. Our hypothetical case involves a decedent who was married shortly before his untimely death. The decedent owned a modest home, a car, a few shares of stock in his employer's company, and a bank account.

Because our decedent was recently married, he had not yet updated his estate plan to allow his estate to pass outside of probate to his wife by survivorship in joint tenancy and community property, or by beneficiary designations on his accounts. All of his property was titled solely in his name at the time of his death. He did not leave a will. (The decedent in this hypothetical case is not unlike many people who put off estate planning until it is too late.)

Affidavit to Collect Wages

Fortunately, probate may still be avoided in this case. Wages or salary due the decedent may be collected by his wife by furnishing to his employer an affidavit that meets a few simple requirements. The affidavit must state that the affiant (the person making the affidavit) is the surviving spouse of the decedent, or is authorized to act on behalf of the spouse, and that no application for the appointment of a personal representative is pending or has been granted (if one was granted, the personal representative must have been discharged, or more than one year must have passed since the filing of a closing statement).

This affidavit may be used any time after the death of the decedent. There is no waiting period. However, payment is limited to $5,000 by the use of this affidavit (not a problem in our hypothetical case).

Affidavit to Collect Personal Property

A separate affidavit must be used to collect the decedent's personal property, such as the money in his bank account, his company stock, and his car. The requirements for this affidavit are different from those for the affidavit to collect wages discussed in the preceding section, but no more difficult. The decedent's spouse must wait 30 days after the decedent's death to use this affidavit.

The affidavit must contain the following statements:
- 30 days have elapsed since the death of the decedent;
- Either: a) an application for the appointment of a personal representative is not pending and a personal representative has not been appointed, and the value of all personal property in the decedent's estate does not exceed $50,000 (as valued as of the date of death), or b) the personal representative has been discharged or more than one year has passed since the filing of a closing statement, and the value of all property in the decedent's estate does not exceed $50,000 (as valued as of the date of the affidavit); and
- The person presenting the affidavit (or on whose

behalf the affidavit is presented) is entitled to the property.

Note that all of the decedent's property, wherever located, must be included in the valuation determination, less liens and encumbrances. When the personal property affidavit is presented by the decedent's wife to the bank, the bank will close the decedent's account and issue a cashier's check to the widow.

Similarly, when the affidavit is presented to the company's stock transfer agent, together with the stock certificate, the stock will be reissued in the widow's name. (It may be more convenient to have a stockbroker handle the stock transfer for a small fee.)

The motor vehicle division will transfer title of the decedent's vehicle to the widow upon presentation of the affidavit and on payment of the necessary fees.

Because the value of the decedent's personal property in our hypothetical case does not exceed $50,000, the decedent's spouse is able to collect all of it by affidavit.

Affidavit to Collect Real Estate

The sole remaining asset in our hypothetical case is the decedent's house. The assessment for the year in which the decedent died showed the full cash value of the property to be $150,000. The decedent owed $125,000 to the mortgage company at the time of his death.

The decedent's spouse can again use an affidavit to acquire title to the property, but she must wait six months to do so. Once the six-month waiting period is over, the decedent's spouse may file in the superior court in the county in which the decedent was domiciled at the time of his death, an affidavit describing the real property and the interest of the decedent in the property. The affidavit must contain specific statements required by the statute, and must have certain documents attached to it. Any false statement in the affidavit may subject the person to penalties for perjury. The real property affidavit does have certain limitations: 1) the value of the property, less all liens and encumbrances, cannot exceed $75,000; 2) the affidavit cannot be used if an application for the appointment of a personal representative is pending or if one has been appointed; 3) the affidavit cannot be filed sooner than six months after the decedent's death; 4) the decedent's funeral expenses and debts must have been be paid; and 5) no estate tax can be due on the decedent's estate.

The requirements for the affidavit are set forth more specifically in A.R.S. Section 14-3971(E), the text of which can be downloaded from the Arizona State Legislature's Web site, www.azleg.gov, or obtained from most public libraries in Arizona.

On receipt of the properly completed affidavit (and any necessary attachments), the probate registrar will issue a certified copy of the affidavit to the filer. The certified copy must then be recorded in the office of the recorder in the county where the real property is located.

As the above hypothetical case illustrates, affidavits can be used in Arizona to collect wages and salaries up to $5,000, to collect personal property up to $50,000, and to transfer title to real property having a net value of not more than $75,000. When affidavits are used in lieu of probate, the cost savings can be considerable.

50

Nonprobate Transfers of Bank Accounts

Avoiding probate by using pay on death designations and survivorship provisions

Checking accounts, savings accounts, certificates of deposit, and credit union share accounts all may be transferred outside of probate. This chapter shows how it can be done.

Pay on Death Designation

A "pay on death" designation[2] means the designation of 1) a beneficiary in an account payable to one party during the party's lifetime and, on the party's death, to one or more beneficiaries; or 2) a beneficiary in an account in the name of one or more parties as trustee for one or more beneficiaries. The second designation is sometimes referred to as "in trust for," but by law it is a pay on death designation.

On the death of the sole party or the last survivor of two or more parties in an account with a pay on death designation, the sums on deposit belong to the surviving beneficiary or beneficiaries. If two or more beneficiaries survive, the money belongs to them in equal shares.

Right of Survivorship

On the death of a party, the sums on deposit in a multiple party account belong to the surviving party or parties. If two or more parties survive and one is the surviving spouse of the deceased party (the "decedent"), the amount to which the decedent, immediately before death, was entitled belongs to the surviving spouse. If two or more parties survive and none is the surviving spouse, the decedent's share belongs to the surviving parties in equal shares. The right of survivorship continues between the surviving parties.

Estate Planning Considerations

The type of account is established by the party or parties owning it.

An account may be changed by written notice given to the financial institution to change the account, or to stop or vary payment under the terms of the account.

As shown above, probate is not necessary to transfer ownership of sums on deposit in an account with a pay on death designation or one with the right of survivorship. Because avoiding probate is desirable, consideration should be given to employing these types of accounts for estate planning purposes.

51

Beneficiary Deeds to Avoid Probate

How to transfer real estate outside of probate

A deed is a legal document that transfers an interest in real estate to another person. Anyone who owns a house acquired title to it by a deed. In this chapter, we will see how real property can be transferred outside of probate by using a beneficiary deed.

A beneficiary deed conveys an interest in real property to another person, called the beneficiary, on the *death* of the property owner. The transfer is subject to all liens and encumbrances on the property at the time of the owner's death. A beneficiary deed can be used by an owner of real property to transfer that property on his death *outside of probate*. A beneficiary deed may designate multiple beneficiaries, and state how those beneficiaries will take title to the property.

If the property is owned by more than one person, all of the owners should sign the beneficiary deed. If the property is owned as joint tenants with the right of survivorship or as community property with the right of survivorship, and all of the owners execute the beneficiary deed, the deed is effective on the death of the last surviving owner. (Special rules apply if less than all of the owners sign the beneficiary deed.)

A beneficiary deed is valid only if it is executed and recorded as provided by law in the office of the county recorder in the county in which the property is located, before the death of the owner or the last surviving owner.

The chief characteristic of a beneficiary deed is that the transfer of the owner's interest in the property is not effective until the owner's death. Thus, the beneficiary does not acquire any interest in the property during the owner's lifetime.

A beneficiary deed may be revoked at any time by the owner or owners who executed it. To be effective, the revocation must be executed and recorded in the county recorder's office before the death of the owner or the last surviving owner, if there are survivorship rights. A beneficiary deed cannot be revoked by the provisions of a will.

Because a beneficiary deed may be used to avoid probate, it should be considered as part of any comprehensive estate plan.

52

Ways to Take Title to Real Estate in Arizona

Taking title has both legal and tax consequences.

When a person buys a house, rental property or vacation home, he takes title to the property. This chapter examines and compares the different ways to take title to real estate in Arizona.

- **Community Property.** To take title as community property, the title holders must have a valid marriage. Each spouse holds an undivided one-half interest in the estate. One spouse cannot partition the property by selling his or her interest. The signatures of both spouses are required to convey title or encumber the property. Each spouse can devise (will) one-half of the community property. Upon death, the estate of the decedent must be "cleared" through probate, affidavit, or adjudication (court action). Both halves of the community property are entitled to a stepped-up tax basis as of the date of death.

- **Joint Tenancy with Right of Survivorship.** The parties need not be married to take title as joint tenants, and there may be more than two joint tenants. Each joint tenant holds an equal and undivided interest in the estate. There is unity of interest. One joint tenant can partition the property by selling his or her joint interest. The signatures of all joint tenants are required to convey or encumber the whole. The estate passes to the surviving tenant or tenants outside of probate. No court action is required to clear title upon the death of a joint tenant. The deceased tenant's share is entitled to a stepped-up tax basis as of the date of death.

- **Community Property with Right of Survivorship.** This method of taking title combines the most favorable characteristics of the first two methods. Because title is taken as community property, the parties must be married. As with the first method (community property *without* the right of survivorship), each spouse holds an undivided one-half interest in the estate, one spouse cannot partition the property by selling his or her interest, and the signatures of both spouses are required to convey title or encumber the property. However, unlike the first method, no court action is required to clear title upon the first death (this feature is common to joint tenancy with right of survivorship). Both halves of the community property are entitled to a stepped-up tax basis as of the date of death.

- **Tenancy in Common.** The parties need not be married to take title as tenants in common, and there may be more than two tenants in common. Each tenant in common holds an undivided fractional interest in the estate. The fractional interests can be disproportionate (*e.g.*, 20% and 80%; 40% and 60%; 20%, 20% and 60%; etc.). Each tenant's share can be conveyed, mortgaged or devised to a third party. The signatures of all of the tenants are required to convey or encumber the whole. Upon death, the tenant's proportionate share passes to his or her heirs. The estate of the decedent must be cleared through probate, affidavit, or adjudication. Each share has its own tax basis.

Arizona is a community property state. Property acquired by a husband and wife is presumed to be community property, unless legally specified differently.

Title may be held as "sole and separate." If a married person acquires title as sole and separate property, his spouse must execute a disclaimer deed to avoid the presumption of community property.

Parties may choose to hold title in the name of an entity. The entity holding title may be a corporation, limited liability company, partnership, or a trust.

Each method of taking title has certain legal and tax consequences. Accordingly, the reader is encouraged to obtain competent legal and tax advice before taking title to his next house, rental property, or vacation home.

53

Lifetime Gifts

"You can't take it with you when you go." —Proverb

Gifts of property may be made by a person during his lifetime, or after his death. This chapter deals with lifetime gifts. Gifts made after death are discussed generally in the chapters on wills and trusts, and nonprobate transfers.

Property is divided into two basic types: personal property and real property. "Personal property" is all property other than real property. "Real property" is synonymous with real estate and interests in real estate. The gift rules are different for each type of property.

Gifts of Personal Property

To make a valid lifetime gift of personal property, the gift must be in writing, duly acknowledged and recorded, or actual possession of the gift must be passed to and remain with the donee (the gift recipient), or someone claiming under him. The rules for making gifts to minors are set forth in Chapter 54.

Gifts of Real Property

To make a valid lifetime gift of real property, the transfer must be by a properly executed deed or instrument of conveyance, and delivered by the party making the gift, or by his authorized agent. Every deed or conveyance of real property must be signed by the donor (the person making the gift) and properly notarized. The deed or instrument of conveyance should be recorded in the office of the county recorder where the property is located.

Gift Tax

A person who makes a gift of property during his lifetime may be subject to federal gift tax. Most gifts are not subject to the gift tax, however. There is usually no tax if the gift is made to a spouse. If a gift is made to someone else, the gift tax does not apply until the value of the gifts to that person is more than the annual exclusion for the year.

A separate annual exclusion applies to each person to whom a gift is made. For gifts made on or after January 1, 2009, the annual exclusion is $13,000 per person. The annual exclusion may be increased in future years due to cost-of-living adjustments. A person contemplating making a gift should consult his tax advisor, or contact the Internal Revenue Service for the current amount of the annual exclusion.

Even if tax applies to a person's gifts, he will generally be able to eliminate or reduce the gift tax by using the so-called unified credit. (We are now getting into tax law, which is beyond the scope of this handbook. For those interested in this subject, the author suggests obtaining a copy of IRS Publication 950, Introduction to Estate and Gift Taxes. This publication may be obtained online from the IRS's Web site, www.irs.gov.

Generally, a person will need to file a gift tax return only if a gift is made to someone other than that person's spouse *and* the value of the gift is more than the gift tax exclusion for that year. A person who receives a gift will not have to pay any gift tax because of it, nor will that person have to pay income tax on the value of the gift.

A person making a gift cannot deduct the value of the gift, unless the gift is made to a qualified charity. In that case, the gift may be a deductible charitable contribution. Here, again, a qualified tax advisor should be consulted before the gift is made.

54

Gifts to Minors

Arizona's Uniform Transfers to Minors Act

Gifts to minors may be made pursuant to the Arizona Uniform Transfers to Minors Act. The Act makes gift-giving to minors relatively easy and inexpensive. This chapter discusses the process of giving gifts to minors under the Act.

A gift to a minor may consist of stock, money, ownership of a life insurance policy or annuity contract, a right to future payments under a contract, an interest in real estate, or a certificate of title to a vehicle. The list is not inclusive, in that an interest in virtually any property may be transferred to a minor under the Act.

The process to transfer property to a minor is fairly simple. The person making the gift appoints an adult (over 21 years of age) or a trust company, as *custodian* for the minor. The custodian then takes control of the property until the minor attains the age of 18 or 21 years (depending on the manner by which the gift was made), or the minor dies. A gift may also be made pursuant to a person's will or trust, or, under certain circumstances, by a person's personal representative or trustee.

The following language must generally be used in connection with the transfer of any property to a custodian: "as custodian for _____ (name of minor) under the Arizona Uniform Transfer to Minors Act." The transfer requirements for different kinds of property are set forth in the statute,

A.R.S. Section 14-7659, which should be consulted prior to any property transfer. (A copy of the statute may be obtained at most public libraries, or online from the Arizona State Legislature's Web site, www.azleg.gov.)

Duties of Custodian

A custodian must take control of the minor's property, register or record title to it if appropriate, and collect, hold, manage, invest and reinvest the property. In dealing with the property (which is referred to as the "custodial property"), a custodian must observe the standard of care that would be observed by a "prudent person" dealing with property of another. If a custodian has a special skill or expertise, he must use it.

A custodian must keep the custodial property separate from all other property, sufficient to identify it clearly as custodial property of the minor. The custodian must also keep records of all transactions with respect to the custodial property. The records must be made available to a parent of the minor, or to the minor if he is at least 14 years of age.

Use of Custodial Property; Custodian's Expenses

A custodian may deliver or pay to the minor, or expend for the minor's benefit, as much of the custodial property as the custodian considers advisable for the minor's use and benefit.

A custodian is entitled to reimbursement from the custodial property for reasonable expenses incurred in the performance of his duties.

Successor Custodian

A person who is nominated to be a custodian may decline to serve. A custodian at any time may designate a trust company or an adult (other than the person who made the gift) as "successor custodian."

A custodian may resign at any time by delivering written notice to the minor (if he is at least 14 years of age) and to the successor custodian. The resigning custodian must deliver the custodial property to the successor custodian. If a custodian dies or becomes incapacitated without having designated a successor, the Act contains rules for the appointment of a successor.

Legal Tip:

Making gifts to minors is an important part of many estate plans. Whenever possible, the gifts should be made pursuant to the Arizona Uniform Transfers to Minors Act, discussed above.

55

Durable Powers of Attorney

"Better be safe than sorry." —Proverb

A durable power of attorney is an important component of any comprehensive estate plan. Simply stated, a durable power of attorney is a document by which one person appoints another person to make financial decisions for him if he is subsequently disabled or incapacitated. Properly executed, it can save both time and money in managing the financial affairs of a person who becomes disabled or incapacitated.

In a durable power of attorney, one person (the "principal") designates another person as his agent. Both the principal and agent must be 18 years of age or older. The document must contain words showing the principal's intent that the authority granted in the durable power of attorney may be exercised if the principal is subsequently disabled or incapacitated, regardless of how much time has elapsed (unless the document states a termination date). A durable power of attorney may become effective upon its execution, or it may become effective upon the principal's disability or incapacity (a so-called "springing" power of attorney).

By executing a written power of attorney, a principal may designate an agent to make financial decisions on the principal's behalf. The power of attorney must contain language that clearly shows the principal intends to create a power of attorney and identifies the agent. It must be signed by the principal (or, in rare cases, by someone else for the principal), and must be properly witnessed and notarized. The witness cannot be the agent, the agent's spouse, the agent's child, or the notary public. (The execution requirements are set forth in A.R.S. Section 14-5501, the text of which is available on the Arizona State Legislature's Web site, www.azleg.gov.)

A person may nominate in a durable power of attorney a conservator or guardian for consideration by the court if protective proceedings for him or his estate are commenced. (For information concerning guardianship and conservatorship proceedings, please see Chapters 58 and 59.)

Any act done by an agent pursuant to a durable power of attorney while the principal is disabled or incapacitated binds the principal as if he were not incapacitated or disabled.

A person who is in a position of trust and confidence to a vulnerable adult must use the vulnerable adult's assets solely for the vulnerable adult's benefit, unless the transaction is specifically authorized in a valid durable power of attorney that is executed by the vulnerable adult as the principal, or unless certain other exceptions apply. An agent who holds a principal's power of attorney and who uses or manages the principal's assets or property with the intent to unlawfully deprive that person of the asset or property is guilty of theft and may be criminally prosecuted.

Some Other Rules:

- A power of attorney executed in another state is valid in Arizona if it was validly executed in the state in which it was created.
- If the agent acted with intimidation or deception in obtaining the power of attorney, he is subject to criminal prosecution and civil penalties.
- A power of attorney is invalid if it was executed by an adult who was incapable of understanding, in a reasonable manner, the nature and effect of his actions.
- A power of attorney may be revoked by the principal.

- A power of attorney may contain a termination date.
- The death of the principal terminates the authority granted to the agent by the document (when the agent learns of the principal's death).
- A durable power of attorney does not establish authority for an agent to make health care decisions for his principal. (This topic is discussed in the next chapter on health care directives).

Legal Tip:

As with other estate planning documents, it is important that the power of attorney be properly drafted and executed. For this reason, an attorney should be consulted to handle the matter. (For the price, it is fairly cheap insurance to protect against drafting and execution errors.)

56

Health Care Directives

"How few of his friends' houses would a man choose to be at when he is sick." —Samuel Johnson

A health care directive is, as the name implies, a document prepared to deal with a person's future health care decisions. In Arizona, there are three types of health care directives: 1) a health care power of attorney, 2) a prehospital medical care directive, and 3) a mental health care power of attorney. A living will, which may be attached to a health care power of attorney or executed separately, is discussed in the next chapter.

Why a chapter on health care directives? The answer is that health care directives constitute an important part of any comprehensive estate plan. Every person implementing an estate plan in Arizona should give serious consideration to executing one or more health care directives.

Each type of directive is discussed below.

1. Health Care Power of Attorney

A health care power of attorney is a written designation of an agent to make health care decisions. It is a durable power of attorney, which means that it survives the person's subsequent disability or incompetency.

A person who is 18 years of age or older (the "principal") may designate another adult (the "agent") to make health care decisions on that person's behalf. The health care power of attorney must meet certain legal requirements, including that it be dated and signed, and notarized or witnessed by at least one adult. The principal must appear to be of sound mind and free from duress at the time the health care power of attorney is signed.

An agent designated in a health care power of attorney has full power to give or refuse consent to all medical, surgical, hospital and related health care. The power of attorney is only effective on the inability of the principal to make or communicate health care decisions. If the principal has also executed a living will, the agent will be directed to implement those choices that the principal initialed in the living will.

An amendment to the power of attorney, unless made only to indicate an agent's change of address or phone number, must meet all of the legal requirements applicable to executing the original document. A health care power of attorney, once made, continues in effect until those who may rely on it have notice of its revocation.

2. Prehospital Medical Care Directive

A prehospital medical care directive is a document that, in the event of cardiac or respiratory arrest by the patient, directs the withholding of cardiopulmonary resuscitation by emergency medical system and hospital emergency department personnel. Withholding of cardiopulmonary resuscitation pursuant to a prehospital medical care directive does not, however, include the withholding of other medical interventions, such as intravenous fluids, oxygen or other therapies deemed necessary to provide comfort care or to alleviate pain.

A prehospital medical care directive must be printed on an orange background and may be in either letter or wallet size. A person who has a valid prehospital medical care directive may wear an identifying bracelet on either his wrist or his ankle. The bracelet must be similar to identification bracelets worn in hospitals, be on an orange background, and state certain information in bold type.

3. *Mental Health Care Power of Attorney*

An adult, known as the principal, may designate another adult or adults, known as the agent, to act as agent and to make mental health care decisions on the principal's behalf. The principal may also designate an alternate adult or adults to act as agent if the original designated agent or agents are unwilling or unable to act.

The agent may make decisions about the mental health treatment on behalf of the principal if the principal is found incapable. If an adult does not have a mental health care power of attorney, an agent with a health care power of attorney (discussed in section 1 above) may make decisions about mental health treatment on behalf of the principal if the principal is found incapable. However, an agent may not consent to admit the principal to a level one behavioral health facility unless the authority is expressly stated in the power of attorney.

The decisions about mental health treatment on behalf of the principal must be consistent with any wishes the principal has expressed in the mental health care directive, mental health care power of attorney, health care power of attorney, or other advance directive.

Note About Legal Requirements for Directives

Due to space limitations, not all of the legal requirements for the health care directives discussed in this chapter have been included. For each type of directive, there are a host of specific requirements that must be followed. The requirements are set forth in Sections 36-3201 through 36-3287 of the Arizona Revised Statutes. For those interested, the text of those statutes may be obtained from the Arizona State Legislature's Web site, www.azleg.gov.

Consistent with the author's advice concerning the drafting and execution of other estate planning documents discussed in this book, the author recommends that an attorney be retained to draft and oversee the execution of all health care directives. By using an attorney, legal compliance will be assured.

57

Living Wills

"One cannot live for ever by ignoring the price of coffins."
—Ernest Bramah

A living will is a written statement by a person intended to guide or control the health care treatment decisions that can be made on his behalf. Contrary to what may be suggested by the name, a living will is not legally related to a *will* or to a *living trust* (although all three documents may be written as part of a comprehensive estate plan).

A person may write and use a living will without writing a health care power of attorney,[3] or may attach a living will to his health care power of attorney. (If the living will is not part of a health care power of attorney, the person must verify it in the same manner as required for a health care power of attorney.) If a person has a health care power of attorney, the agent must make health care decisions that are consistent with the person's known desires and that are medically reasonable and appropriate. A person can, but is not required to, state his desires in a living will.

In a typical living will, the person writing it will answer the following basic questions relating to his health care:

- If you have a terminal condition, do you *not* want your life to be prolonged and do you *not* want life-sustaining treatment, beyond comfort care, that would serve only to artificially delay the moment of your death?

- If you are in a terminal condition or an irreversible coma or a persistent vegetative state that your doctors reasonably feel to be irreversible or incurable, do you want the medical treatment necessary to provide care that would keep you comfortable, but *not* cardiopulmonary resuscitation, artificially administered food and fluids, and/or to be taken to a hospital if at all avoidable?
- (For women only) If you are known to be pregnant, do you want life-sustaining treatment used if it is possible that the embryo/fetus will develop to the point of live birth with the continued application of life-sustaining treatment?
- Do you want the use of all medical care necessary to treat your condition until your doctors reasonably conclude that your condition is terminal or is irreversible and incurable or you are in a persistent vegetative state?
- Do you want your life to be prolonged to the greatest extent possible?

A person writing a living will is free to make other or additional statements of desires, and attach additional special provisions or limitations to the document. In that a living will is intended to guide or control the health care treatment decisions that can be made on that person's behalf, it should be as specific and personal as possible.

58

Guardianships

"Thy brother's keeper." —Bible: Genesis 4

A guardian is a person appointed by the court to guard the health, safety and welfare of another. A guardian may be appointed for a minor (anyone under the age of 18), or for an incapacitated person. The term "incapacitated person" is defined by law to mean any person who is impaired by reason of mental illness, mental deficiency, mental disorder, physical illness or disability, chronic use of drugs, chronic intoxication or other cause, except minority, to the extent that he lacks sufficient understanding or capacity to make or communicate responsible decisions concerning himself. The person for whom a guardian is appointed is called the "ward."

Generally speaking, a guardian has the same powers and authority over a ward that a parent has over a child. The guardian may, for instance, consent to medical treatment and other professional services for the ward. The guardian may also consent to psychiatric and psychological care. When it comes to the *property* of the ward, however, the guardian has very limited powers. If the ward has property in need of management or protection, a conservator should be appointed. A "conservator" is a person appointed to protect the property of a disabled person. (Conservatorships are discussed in the next chapter.) In some cases, the ward needs both a guardian and a conservator, which may or may not be the same person.

Guardian of a Minor

A parent of a minor can, by last will and testament, appoint a guardian for his or her child. In order for this so-called testamentary appointment to become effective: 1) both parents must be dead; or 2) the surviving parent's parental rights must have been terminated; or 3) the surviving parent must be incapacitated. Otherwise, the surviving parent will have the care and custody of the child (even if the parents are divorced, and the deceased parent was awarded sole custody). If the minor child is 14 years of age or older, the child may object to the appointment of the guardian. If the child objects, the court will base the appointment on "the welfare and best interests of the minor."

The court may appoint a guardian for an unmarried minor if both parents are dead or their rights to custody have been terminated or suspended by circumstances or court order. Any person whose appointment would be in the best interests of the minor may be appointed. In most cases, this likely will be a relative of the minor. If the court appoints a guardian because the parents are unable or unwilling to care for their child, the guardianship may be terminated upon a change of those circumstances.

Guardian of an Incapacitated Person

A guardian for an incapacitated person may be appointed by will of a parent or spouse, or by court order. Most often appointment is by court order. Court appointment of a guardian for an incapacitated person involves a judicial proceeding. Notice of the proceeding must be given to the person alleged to be incapacitated and to all other persons who have a legal interest in the outcome, such as a spouse, parents and adult children. The court will hold a hearing on the issue of incapacity. To protect the rights of the alleged incapacitated person, the court will appoint an attorney to represent the person, an investigator to investigate the allegations concerning the person, and a physician to examine the person. The court will appoint a guardian only if it is satisfied, after considering all the evidence, that the person is incapacitated and in need of a guardian.

The court retains jurisdiction over all guardianship proceedings. The guardian is, thus, accountable to the court for all actions on behalf of the ward, until the guardian's resignation, removal or termination of appointment.

59

Conservatorships

*A conservator manages the property of a minor
or disabled adult.*

A conservator is a person who acts as a trustee of another person's property. If a minor (a person under 18) or a disabled adult owns property that needs protection and management, a conservator should be appointed. The same person may serve as a conservator and guardian. (For a discussion concerning guardianships, please refer to the preceding chapter.)

A conservatorship proceeding may be started by an elderly person who desires protection of his or her property, or by any person interested in the estate, affairs or welfare of the disabled person. The disability may be mental or physical. Missing persons and prisoners of war are considered disabled persons under the conservatorship statutes.

There is no requirement that an adult be declared "incompetent" in order for a conservator to be appointed. The test for disability is whether or not the adult is able to manage his or her property and affairs effectively. The court, depending on the nature of the alleged disability, may appoint a physician to examine the person and an investigator to investigate the issue of disability.

Once a conservatorship petition is filed, notice must be given to certain persons whose interests may be affected by the outcome of the proceeding. Those persons include a spouse, a guardian, parents and children. Any interested person may participate in the proceeding, and may file a demand for notice. If a demand for notice is filed, the person filing the demand will receive notice of all events and copies of all court papers in the proceeding.

In a conservatorship proceeding, the court *may* appoint an attorney to represent the minor, and *must* appoint an attorney to represent the adult if he does not have counsel of his own. The appointment of counsel is to ensure that the alleged disabled person's rights are protected.

The conservator must furnish a bond to ensure the faithful performance of his duties. The court determines the amount of the bond based on the circumstances of each case, although the bond amount generally will be equal to the value of the property in the conservator's control, plus one-year's estimated income (*i.e.,* interest, dividends and benefits), minus the value of any assets that the conservator lacks the power to sell or convey without court authorization. The conservator's bond is subject to periodic review, and the amount may be adjusted by the court from time to time. A conservator's bond may be purchased from most insurance companies.

The conservator is vested with legal title to all property of the protected person. The court-issued Letters of Conservatorship are evidence of the authority of the conservator. The conservator has the power to sell, buy, lease, transfer, encumber or otherwise dispose of the property of the protected person. The exercise of these broad powers is subject to fiduciary duties and the same standard of care applicable to trustees. When in doubt regarding a particular transaction or course of action, the conservator may ask the court for instructions.

The conservator must file an inventory of the protected person's assets within 90 days after the conservator's appointment. The conservator must account to the court annually, and also on termination. The accounts must contain details concerning all income and expenses during the accounting period, gains and losses on assets, and other information relating to the value of the estate. If the conservator is requesting attorney's fees be paid from the estate, a petition for approval of attorney's fees must also be filed.

A conservator may resign by petitioning the court, or may be removed for good cause. If the conservator resigns, is removed, or dies, the court may appoint a successor conservator.

The conservatorship should terminate: 1) in the case of a minor, when the minor reaches age 18 (assuming no other disability); 2) in the case of a disabled adult, when the disability has ceased; and 3) in all cases, when the protected person dies. Upon termination of the conservatorship, title to the assets passes to the person for whom the conservator was appointed, or if that person is deceased, to his estate.

PART FIVE

Civil Lawsuits and Claims

60

Civil Lawsuits in Arizona

"A lawsuit is civilized warfare." —Legal maxim

In Arizona, about 100,000 civil actions are filed each year. A civil action generally is filed in the superior court. If the amount in controversy is $10,000 or less, it may be filed in a justice court (see Chapter 82). This chapter looks at the structure of a civil action brought in the Arizona Superior Court.

What is a Civil Action?

A civil action, simply defined, is a lawsuit brought to enforce, restore or protect private rights. Most commonly, a civil action is brought for monetary relief. Most civil actions involve claims arising out of breach of contract, motor vehicle accidents, malpractice, or other negligence. The terms "civil action" and "lawsuit" are interchangeable, as both refer to an action or proceeding in a civil court.

Starting a Lawsuit

The filing of a complaint with the clerk of the court starts a lawsuit. A complaint is a formal written statement filed by the party who starts the lawsuit (the plaintiff), which asserts that party's claims in the action. When a complaint is filed, the case is assigned a number by the clerk. The clerk issues a summons, which is an official court document that requires the other party (the defendant) to defend against the plaintiff's claims as stated in the complaint. A summons is served upon the defendant with a copy of the complaint.[1]

Once served, a defendant must file a written response to the allegations made by the plaintiff in the complaint. An answer may be accompanied by a counterclaim, which asserts claims by the defendant against the plaintiff. The time for responding to the plaintiff's complaint depends upon a number of factors, including whether service was made within or outside the state of Arizona.

A defendant personally served with a summons and complaint within the state of Arizona has 20 days after service to file a response with the court. If the defendant fails to respond within the required time, a default will be entered against the defendant and the plaintiff may be granted a judgment for the relief requested in the complaint. This is known as a "default judgment."

Every civil action is assigned to a judge at the beginning of the case. Each side is entitled to one change of judge as a matter of right. The right is exercised by the filing of a notice of change of judge.

Pretrial Procedures

Disclosure of Information

Each party must furnish to the other a written disclosure of information within 40 days after the defendant's answer is filed. This disclosure statement, as it is called, must contain specific information concerning the claims and defenses, the identities of witnesses, a description of all exhibits, and other pertinent information prescribed by Arizona Court Rule 26.1. The failure to disclose the information required by this court rule will result in penalties against the non-complying party, which may include exclusion of undisclosed evidence at the time of trial.

Alternative Dispute Resolution

Upon motion of any party, or upon its own initiative after consultation with the parties, the court may direct the parties to submit the dispute to an alternative dispute resolution program created or authorized by the court. In any event, no later than 90 days following the first appearance of a defendant, the parties must confer, either in person or by telephone, about the possibilities for a prompt settlement of the case, or whether they might benefit from participating in some form of alternative dispute resolution. Within 30 days after their conference, the parties are required to inform the court regarding their willingness to participate in alternative dispute resolution. If they agree to use alternative dispute resolution methods, the court will enter appropriate orders.

Discovery

Any party in a civil action may use discovery procedures to uncover evidence and avoid the element of surprise at the time of trial. The primary purpose of discovery is to uncover evidence. Discovery may also be used, however, to preserve evidence, to narrow issues, to secure admissions, and to confine testimony. The parties conduct discovery to prepare their cases for trial.

Under the rules of civil procedure, the various discovery procedures available are: oral depositions, written questions and interrogatories, requests to produce documents and things, physical and mental examinations, and requests for admission. The use of one discovery procedure does not preclude the use of others, and there is no required sequence for their use.

Illustration: Prior to trial, one party wants to take the deposition of the other party. The party desiring the deposition sends the other party a notice of deposition, specifying the place, date and time of the deposition. The party taking the deposition will be allowed to ask the other party a wide range of questions regarding the claims and defenses in the lawsuit. The testimony is given under oath and in the presence of a court reporter. The transcript of the deposition may be used at the time of trial to help prove or disprove any claim or defense in the case. If the person giving the deposition changes his or her testimony at the trial, the deposition can be used to show the changed testimony.

Compulsory Arbitration

Local Limits

The superior court in each county is authorized by law to require arbitration of all matters where the amount in controversy does not exceed $65,000. In most counties, however, the limits set by local rule for required arbitration are considerably less than $65,000.

In every case, the plaintiff must file a certificate with the complaint indicating whether the case is subject to compulsory arbitration under the local rule of the court in which the case is filed. If a defendant disagrees with the plaintiff's certificate, the defendant must file a controverting certificate with the answer.

Appointment of Arbitrator

Cases that are subject to arbitration are placed on the arbitration calendar. The court administrator then selects an attorney from a list of attorneys to serve as the arbitrator in the case. Either side may file one notice of strike within 10 days after the arbitrator is appointed, in which event another attorney will be selected from the court administrator's list to serve as the arbitrator.

Arbitration Hearing

The court-appointed arbitrator is empowered to swear witnesses and conduct the hearing. An arbitrator generally schedules the arbitration hearing (which most often is held at the arbitrator's office) shortly after he or she is appointed as the arbitrator in a case. The rules of evidence are somewhat relaxed in the arbitration proceedings, and certain evidence is admissible at the hearing without the usual requirements. The arbitrator files an arbitration award with the court after the hearing has concluded. The arbitration award determines which party, if any, is entitled to money from the other.

Appeal From Arbitration

Any party who appears and participates in the arbitration hearing may contest the arbitration award. To do so, the party contesting the award must file an appeal with the clerk of the court within 20 days after the arbitration award is filed, and request that the case be set for trial in the superior court. At the time of filing the notice of appeal, the party appealing from the award must deposit with the clerk of the court a sum equal to one hearing day's compensation of the arbitrator, but not exceeding 10% of the amount in controversy. The trial is a new determination of all issues in the case. Either party may request a jury trial.

The deposit on appeal will be refunded to the party appealing from the arbitration award if he obtains a judgment on the trial that is at least 23% more favorable than the award. If the judgment on the trial is not more favorable by at least 23% than the monetary relief granted by the arbitration award, the court will order the deposit to be used to pay the costs and fees related to the appeal. If the deposit is insufficient to pay all the costs and fees on appeal, the court will, absent a showing of substantial economic hardship, require the party appealing from the award to pay the difference.

Illustration: A plaintiff who appeals from a $10,000 award must obtain a judgment of at least $12,300 to avoid paying the defendant's attorney fees and costs on appeal. Conversely, to avoid paying the plaintiff's attorney fees and costs on appeal, a defendant who appeals from a $10,000 award cannot have a judgment entered against him for more than $7,700.

If no appeal has been filed by the expiration of the time for appeal, any party may file to have a judgment entered on the award. If no application for entry of judgment is filed within 120 days from the date of the arbitrator's decision and no appeal is pending, the case will be dismissed.

Most cases that are subject to compulsory arbitration are resolved in the arbitration proceedings and do not go to trial. Arbitration is a preferred method of resolving disputes.

Setting a Case for Trial

A case that is not subject to arbitration gets set for trial by the filing of a Motion to Set and Certificate of Readiness. This is a court document that requests the assigned judge to set the case for trial and certifies that all discovery has been completed or will be completed in advance of trial. If one party disagrees with the other party's Motion to Set and Certificate of Readiness, the party in disagreement may file a controverting certificate with the court. The trial judge will then decide whether the case is ready to be set for trial.

When a case is ready to be set for trial, the trial judge may set a pretrial conference before setting a trial date, or may schedule both at the same time. Any party may request a trial by jury. If a jury trial is not requested, the trial will be by the judge.

If neither party files a Motion to Set and Certificate of Readiness within nine months from the commencement of the action, the case will be placed on the inactive calendar. A case that remains on the inactive calendar for two months may be dismissed for lack of prosecution. These fast-track time periods are shorter than the time periods in most other courts outside Arizona, and result in cases being decided here more quickly than in most other jurisdictions.

Motions

At any time during the pendency of a civil action, a party may file a motion, or a formal written request asking the court for some form of relief. Motions made during a trial may be oral. If a claim is not well grounded in fact or law, the opposing party may file a motion to dismiss before trial. If a motion to dismiss is granted, the claim will be dismissed without a trial.

Illustration: The defendant files a motion to dismiss the plaintiff's personal injury claim because it was filed more than two years after the accident happened. The statute of limitations is two years. The court grants the defendant's motion, and the plaintiff's case is dismissed without a trial.

The Trial

In Arizona, civil trial juries consist of eight members (most readers probably would have guessed 12). The number of jurors is set by state law, but can be changed by agreement of the parties and the judge. In some cases, the parties stipulate to a lesser or greater number of jurors.

Regardless of the number of jurors, each juror must be a citizen of the U.S., be a resident of the county in which he or she is summoned to serve, be free of a felony conviction, and not be mentally incompetent or insane.

After a jury has been impaneled in a civil case, the attorneys[2] may make opening statements. Following opening statements, the case proceeds as follows: a) the plaintiff's evidence is introduced, b) the defendant's evidence is introduced, c) the plaintiff may offer rebuttal evidence, and d) the defendant may offer rebuttal evidence.

The attorneys make closing arguments after all the evidence has been presented. The court then instructs the jury on the law and the case is submitted to the jury for deliberations. Unless the parties otherwise agree, at least six of the eight jurors must support the jury's decision. The jury's decision is called a verdict. The verdict does not have to be unanimous, so long as the required number of jurors have voted in favor of the verdict. The court will enter a judgment in the case based on the verdict, unless it is contrary to law. In cases tried by the judge, the judge acts as a one-person jury.

Award of Fees and Costs

The successful party in a civil action is awarded costs, but not necessarily attorney fees. In order for the winning party to recover attorney fees, there must be a legal basis. In Arizona, one such basis is a statute that allows attorney fees to be awarded to the successful party in any action arising out of a contract. Another basis, previously mentioned, is the arbitration rule that requires a party who unsuccessfully appeals from an arbitration award to pay the other party's costs and attorney fees.

The amount of attorney fees awarded to the successful party is determined by the judge, and not the jury.

Appeals

After the trial, the losing party may file post-trial motions requesting that the judgment be vacated or that the jury's verdict not be followed, and may appeal from the judgment to the courts of appeal. However, the decision of the trial judge will be affirmed unless material mistakes were made during the trial. In the vast majority of appeals, the trial court's judgment is upheld. The losing party on appeal may be ordered by the court of appeals to pay the winning party's attorney fees on appeal in appropriate cases.

61

The Law of Torts

"It is difficult to imagine a human activity that is not subject to the law of torts."

This chapter was written for those who think a tort is: a) a dessert that is served at the end of a multi-course meal; b) a game of chance; or c) just another legal four-letter word used by lawyers to confuse non-lawyers.

Actually, a tort is a civil action for damages relating to a variety of injuries. The law of torts is concerned with the allocation of losses arising out of human activities; to afford compensation for injuries sustained by one person as the result of the conduct of another.

Tort Claims

Motor vehicle accident cases comprise the single largest number of tort cases. In the Arizona Superior Court, for instance, approximately two-thirds of the tort cases filed arise out of motor vehicle accidents. The remaining tort cases filed involve claims of medical malpractice, assault, battery, conversion, false imprisonment, intentional infliction of emotional distress, defamation, invasion of privacy, misrepresentation, malicious prosecution, interference with business relations, premises liability, and product liability. (Different types of tort claims are discussed in other chapters of this book).

Some of the torts mentioned in the preceding paragraph

are also crimes, such as assault and battery. A tort is not the same thing as a crime, although the two sometimes have many features in common. A crime is an offense against the public at large, for which the state, as the representative of the people, will bring proceedings in the form of a criminal prosecution. The purpose of a criminal proceeding is to protect and vindicate the interests of the public as a whole, usually by punishing the offender. The civil action for a tort, on the other hand, is maintained by the injured person himself. Its purpose is to compensate him for the damages he has suffered, at the expense of the wrongdoer (also known as the tortfeasor). If the injured party is successful, he will receive a judgment for a sum of money, which he may then enforce against the tortfeasor.

Liability Insurance

In many cases, insurance is available to pay a money judgment entered against a tortfeasor. Auto and homeowners' policies are the two most common types of tort insurance policies in effect today. Both cover negligent acts committed by the policyholder. Most professionals also have professional liability insurance to cover work-related negligence. This type of insurance is commonly referred to as malpractice insurance, and most doctors, lawyers and accountants carry it.

Under almost all insurance policies covering torts, in addition to paying damages, the insurance company must provide a defense for its policyholder in any civil action brought against him. This means that insurance companies hire and pay for the defense attorneys in almost all tort cases.

Contingency Fees

In the vast majority of tort cases, the plaintiff, *i.e.*, the person who claims injury by the wrongful act or conduct of another, is represented by an attorney on a contingent-fee basis. When the fee is contingent, the attorney receives a pre-determined percentage of the amount recovered as his fee in the case. Conversely, if there is no recovery, there is no attorney's fee.

It is widely believed that the contingency fee holds the keys to the courthouse doors for this country's poor and middle class. The Florida Supreme Court has stated, "...the poor and the least fortunate in our society enjoy access to our courts, in part, because of the existence of the contingency fee."

Regardless of whether a fee is contingent, it must be reasonable. The State Bar of Arizona requires that all contingent fee contracts be in writing, and that the fee be reasonable under the circumstances of the case.

Tort Awards

The median award received by injured plaintiffs in large U.S. counties is $30,500, according to a recent U.S. Department of Justice study. This includes both compensatory and punitive damages. Compensatory damages compensate the plaintiff for losses caused by the tortfeasor's negligent or wrongful conduct, while punitive damages punish for a tortfeasor's egregious misconduct and willful or malicious acts. Punitive damages are awarded in only 3% of tort trials won by plaintiffs. And, according to the study, the median punitive damage award for outrageous misconduct is only $38,000. In every case, the trial judge has the power to reduce the jury's damage award if he or she believes it is excessive. The "Headline Awards" of millions of dollars are clearly the exception to the rule in tort cases.

Scope of Law

The law of torts covers a wide range of human activities. Indeed, its scope is so broad it is difficult to imagine a human activity that is not covered by this branch of the law. Thus, a person who sustains injury to his person or property as a result of somebody else's act or conduct, whether it be negligent or intentional, likely has a claim for damages based on the law of torts.

The reader is invited to visit the author's Web site, www. loosebrown.com, for information concerning actual tort cases handled by the author's law firm.

62

Negligence Cases

The failure to use reasonable care

Negligence is the failure to use *reasonable care*. A driver who rear-ends a vehicle in front of him likely is guilty of negligence. In deciding whether a particular action or inaction is negligent, a jury will necessarily determine if the person acted as a "reasonably careful person would have acted under the circumstances." The occurrence of an accident does not, by itself, mean that a particular person has been negligent. In cases involving traffic accidents, defective and dangerous products, unsafe premises, medical malpractice and certain business transactions, the law of negligence is used to determine fault.

Sudden Emergency

In determining whether a person acted with reasonable care under the circumstances, the jury will consider whether the conduct was affected by an emergency. If a person, without negligence on his part, encountered an emergency and acted reasonably to avoid harm to himself or others, he should not be found negligent. This is so, even though, in hindsight, some other or better course of conduct could and should have been followed.

Violation of Law

A person who violates a statute enacted for the protection and safety of the public (*e.g.*, a traffic law), is guilty of negligence. This is known as negligence *per se*, meaning that the mere violation of the law amounts to negligence. Thus, a driver who fails to control his speed to avoid colliding with another vehicle, in violation of the traffic statute regulating speed, is guilty of negligence. Similarly, a driver under the influence of alcohol is guilty of negligence *per se*. (If a driver had a blood alcohol concentration of .08 percent or more at the time of driving, it will be presumed that he was under the influence of alcohol.)

Negligence of a Child

A child is not held to the same standard of care as an adult. A child who does not use the degree of care that is ordinarily exercised by children of the same age, intelligence, knowledge, and experience under the existing circumstances is negligent. An adult must anticipate the behavior of children, and that children might not exercise the same degree of care for their own safety as adults.

Liability for Damages

A person who files a lawsuit for negligence is seeking an award of damages against the negligent person. If a person's negligence is a cause of another person's injury, that person will be at fault. The person at fault is liable for the other person's damages. The measure of damages will, of course, vary from case to case. The jury or judge will decide the amount of money damages in a negligence case.

63

Medical Malpractice

"The blunders of a doctor are felt not by himself but by others." —Ar-Rumi

Medical malpractice is negligence by a health care provider. (Included within the definition of a health care provider are physicians, nurses, physician's assistants, dentists, chiropractors, hospitals, and health care clinics.) Medical negligence means that the health care provider failed to exercise that degree of care, skill, and learning that would be expected of a reasonable, prudent health care provider in the profession or class to which he belongs within the state of Arizona, acting in the same or similar circumstances.

Standard of Care

The Arizona statute adopts a statewide standard of care for all health care providers. Thus, a family practice doctor in one city or town is held to the same standard of care as a family practice doctor in any other city or town in Arizona. (For ease of reference, the terms "doctor" and "health care provider" may be used interchangeably.)

A doctor has a duty to refer a patient to another doctor or to a specialist if the standard of care requires such a referral under the circumstances.

A doctor who undertakes diagnosis or treatment outside his recognized field of practice is required to comply with the standard of care for physicians practicing in the field of medicine in which the diagnosis or treatment is undertaken.

Burden of Proof

In a medical malpractice case, the patient has the burden of proof. The party who has the burden of proof must persuade the jury, by the evidence, that the claim is more probably true than not true. This means that the evidence favoring the patient must outweigh the opposing evidence.

In medical malpractice cases involving certain treatment a) rendered in an emergency department, b) rendered by on-call providers, or c) related to the emergency delivery of infants, the patient must persuade the jury by the evidence that the claim is highly probable. This standard is more exacting than the standard of more probably true than not true, but it is less exacting than the standard of proof beyond a reasonable doubt.

In every case, the patient must prove that his doctor failed to comply with the standard of care. To prove this element, the patient must retain a standard of care expert. This expert will be a doctor familiar with the required standard of care, who will testify on behalf of the patient at trial. The doctor being sued undoubtedly will also have a standard of care expert testify on his behalf. (In the author's experience, the experts rarely agree on much of anything, yet alone the applicable standard of care.) It is up to the jury to decide the winner in the "battle of the experts."

Before a doctor can be found at fault, the patient must also prove that the doctor's negligence was a cause of his injury. The patient may also use an expert witness to prove this element of his claim. Negligence causes an injury if it helps produce the injury, and if the injury would not have happened without the negligence.

Damages

If a doctor is found to be at fault for medical negligence, he will be ordered to pay damages to his patient. The amount of damages will take into account the nature, extent and duration of the injury, the pain and suffering experienced by the patient, the patient's medical expenses, and the patient's lost earnings. If the patient has received any medical or disability benefits, the jury may consider that evidence in evaluating the patient's claim for damages. If the patient is married, the patient's spouse may be awarded damages for loss of love, care, affection, companionship and other pleasures of the marital relationship.

In any trial involving a claim for future damages arising out of medical malpractice, any party may elect to receive or pay future damages for economic losses in periodic installments. There are rules governing the election to pay or receive future damages in installments.

Qualified Immunity

A health professional who provides medical or dental treatment at a nonprofit clinic where neither the professional nor the clinic receives compensation for the treatment generally is not liable for medical malpractice, unless the professional was grossly negligent. A health professional who provides previously owned prescription eyeglasses free of charge through a charitable, nonprofit or fraternal organization generally is not liable for injury to the recipient if: 1) the recipient has signed a medical malpractice release form, and 2) the injury was not a direct result of the health professional's intentional misconduct or gross negligence.

Legal Tip

If you are the victim of medical malpractice, you must generally file a lawsuit against the negligent health care provider within two years from when the malpractice occurred, or when you discovered or reasonably should have discovered the malpractice. If a lawsuit is not filed within this two-year period, it will be barred by the statute of limitations. There are shorter time periods and claim requirements for malpractice actions against public entities and public employees.

64

Motor Vehicle Accidents

"The economic cost of traffic crashes in Arizona is nearly $3 billion per year." — Arizona Department of Transportation

A terrible toll is taken each year in injuries and deaths caused by motor vehicle accidents. In Arizona, approximately 1,000 people lose their lives each year in traffic accidents. The economic cost of traffic crashes in Arizona is nearly $3 billion per year, according to a recent Arizona Department of Transportation report. Given these facts, it is hardly surprising that motor vehicle accidents comprise the single largest number of tort case filings in the Arizona Superior Court.

The law of negligence governs motor vehicle accident cases. (For a detailed discussion concerning the law of negligence, please refer to Chapter 62.) This means that if a person involved in an accident failed to use reasonable care under the circumstances, that person is liable for the damages resulting from the accident.

A person who is injured in a motor vehicle accident is entitled to damages for pain and suffering, disability, permanent impairment, medical bills, lost wages, and property damage. The spouse of an injured party may be entitled to damages for loss of consortium, which is the loss of marital love, affection and services. If the traffic accident resulted in a death, the survivors of the person killed may bring an action for wrongful death. The amount of damages can be determined by agreement between the parties or, if the parties are unable to reach agreement, by the court. By law, the amount must fairly compensate the injured party for his or her damages.

Motor vehicle accidents generally are investigated by the law enforcement agency having jurisdiction over the location. If the accident occurs within Arizona on an Interstate Highway or state route, the accident will be investigated by the Arizona Department of Public Safety. If the accident occurs on a surface street or road within a city, town or village, it will be investigated by the local municipality's police agency. If the accident occurs on an Indian reservation, it will be investigated by the tribal police. If the accident occurs anywhere else in Arizona, it will be investigated by the Sheriff of the county in which it occurs.

Regardless of which agency conducts the accident investigation, the investigating officer will prepare a standard written report of the accident. The traffic accident report is a public record, and a copy of it may be obtained by any interested person upon written request and the payment of a small fee (the amount of which varies among agencies). The traffic accident report may contain evidence of negligence on the part of one or more drivers involved in the accident.

The admission by a driver at the scene of the accident that he or she was at fault is admissible evidence in a civil action. The accident report may contain admissions of fault, as the investigating officer generally questions the drivers at the scene. The officer's recorded personal observations concerning the accident—such as the length of skid marks and measurements of the intersection—are also admissible. However, the officer's opinions and conclusions about the accident generally are inadmissible, as is evidence of a traffic citation.

The violation of a motor vehicle statute can amount to negligence. This is called negligence *per se*. In Arizona, any of the following types of conduct while driving constitute negligence *per se*: excessive speed, driving while intoxicated, failure to yield to a pedestrian in a crosswalk, failure to yield the right-of-way, driving over the center line, failure to use high-beam headlights, and failing to signal a turn or suddenly decreasing speed.

Although violation of a motor vehicle statute can constitute negligence *per se*, the violation must be proved independently in a civil action by showing that the conduct occurred. The fact of a traffic citation or conviction is not admissible to prove the conduct or violation. In addition, a driver's past driving record is not admissible to prove the driver's negligence.

The laws regulating motor vehicles do not apply only to automobiles and trucks. Motorcycles are also vehicles, and bicycles are considered vehicles when operated on a roadway, shoulder or bike path. The rights and duties of pedestrians are also found, in part, in the motor vehicle statutes.

The negligence of the injured person may be asserted by the defendant (the driver being sued) to reduce the defendant's liability. This concept is known as comparative negligence, and reflects the reality that vehicular accidents are not always caused by the sole fault of a single party. The injured party's damages will be reduced by the percentage of that party's fault.

Illustration: Car A fails to yield the right-of-way to Car B, and a collision ensues. However, Car B was exceeding the posted speed, and its speed contributed to the accident. If the driver of Car B was 25% at fault and is awarded damages in the amount of $10,000, the damage award will be reduced by 25%, to $7,500. This is how comparative negligence is applied in cases involving motor vehicle accidents.

In Arizona, a person injured in a motor vehicle accident may not recover damages for injuries which were avoidable by the use of a safety belt or, in the case of a motorcyclist, by the use of a safety helmet. (For a detailed discussion on the use of seat belts and motorcycle helmets, please refer to Chapter 4.) The rationale behind this rule is that a person should not be permitted to recover damages for avoidable consequences.

In certain cases, a non-driver may be found liable for vehicular injuries. For instance, an employer can be held liable for the negligence of an employee. The employee must be acting within the course and scope of his or her employment for the employer to be liable, however. This is the doctrine of *respondeat superior*.

Under the theory of negligent entrustment, the owner of a vehicle may be held liable for negligently entrusting the vehicle to another. The "family purpose doctrine" renders liable one who provides a vehicle to a child for operation by the child, even if the use was for the driver's own pleasure or business. An owner might also be liable based on a statute forbidding the owner to permit the operation of a vehicle which is in an unsafe condition.

Drivers who mix alcohol and gasoline may be liable for *punitive damages* in a civil action (after they serve their jail time for DUI). Punitive damages may be assessed against a drunk driver as punishment for outrageous conduct, such as where the level of the driver's intoxication is particularly high. (A driver is presumed intoxicated if his or her blood alcohol level is tested at .08 or above.) Punitive damages may also be awarded against an employer whose employee caused an accident while intoxicated, under the doctrine of *respondeat superior*. Driving while intoxicated constitutes negligence *per se*.

Motor vehicle accidents are an unfortunate reality of our motorized society. A person involved in one should notify his insurance company immediately. Every auto policy requires the insured to promptly notify his insurance company of the accident and to cooperate in the investigation of the loss. Failure to comply with these requirements may result in a denial of coverage by the insurance company.

Generally, a lawsuit must be filed within two years from the date of the accident or the claim will be barred by the statute of limitations. There are shorter limitation periods and pre-litigation claim procedures in some cases, and legal counsel should be consulted as soon as possible after an accident to confirm the applicable limitations period and legal requirements.

65

Vehicle Owners' Liability

"Here's another fine mess you've gotten me into." —Oliver Hardy

There are certain cases in which the owner of a vehicle may be liable for someone else's use of his vehicle. This chapter discusses those situations.

Negligent Entrustment

An owner may be held liable for negligently entrusting his vehicle to another. The central requirement is that the owner who gives permission to use his vehicle knows that the driver is incompetent to operate it. Thus, an owner who gives permission to an obviously intoxicated person to use his vehicle will be liable for the driver's actions. Applying the same rule, a car rental company will be liable for an accident caused by a driver known by the company to be unlicensed.

Employer's Liability

An employer who provides a vehicle to an employee to perform his job duties or to run a special errand, will be held liable for that employee's actions. This liability is based on the doctrine of *respondeat superior*, which is discussed in greater detail in Chapter 95.

Family Purpose Doctrine

The head of a family who provides a vehicle to a child, regardless of age, may be liable for the child's operation of that vehicle. This is known as the family purpose doctrine. The doctrine applies even if the use of the vehicle is for the child's own pleasure or business. A parent will be deemed to have furnished a vehicle to the child if he physically provides the vehicle, or if he provides the financial resources for the child to purchase the vehicle.

Unlicensed Minor

An owner of a vehicle who knowingly permits an unlicensed minor to drive his vehicle is liable with the minor for damages caused by the minor's negligence or willful misconduct while driving the vehicle. This also applies to a person who gives or furnishes a vehicle to an unlicensed minor, even if the person does not own the vehicle.

66

Wrongful Death Actions

"The survivors...may bring a lawsuit for wrongful death."

Tragically, about a thousand people die each year in auto-mobile accidents on Arizona highways. The survivors of those persons may have wrongful death claims under Arizona law. In this chapter, we will examine the law governing wrongful death.

The survivors of a person whose death was the fault of another may bring a lawsuit for wrongful death. For a wrongful death action to exist, the deceased person (the "decedent") must have had a valid personal injury claim. This means that the person causing the death would have been at fault if death had not occurred. The corollary to this rule is that if the person causing the death would not have been at fault if death had not occurred, there is no liability for wrongful death.

Illustration: The driver of Big Car causes an accident in which one person is injured and another killed. The injured person has an action for personal injury, and the survivors of the person killed have an action for wrongful death. If the driver of Big Car was not at fault in causing the accident, however, the injured person would not have an action for personal injury and the survivors of the person killed would not have an action for wrongful death.

The Arizona Wrongful Death Statute provides that a wrongful death action must be brought by the surviving husband or wife, child, parent or guardian, or personal representative of the decedent. If the decedent is a child, the action may be brought by either parent. The person bringing the action is called the plaintiff, but the action is pursued for the benefit of the beneficiaries. The beneficiaries on whose behalf the action is pursued are the surviving spouse, the children, and the parents of the decedent, or if none of these survive, the decedent's estate.

In a wrongful death action, there is a single recovery by the plaintiff on behalf of all the beneficiaries, identified in the above paragraph. The recovery will be allocated among the beneficiaries according to the loss suffered by each. If the recovery is on behalf of the decedent's estate, the money will be distributed according to the decedent's will or, if there is no will, according to the laws of intestate succession (i.e., the laws governing how property is distributed in the absence of a will, discussed in Chapter 48).

In a wrongful death action, the jury must give such damages as it deems "fair and just." The amounts recovered are not subject to debts or liabilities of the deceased, unless the action is brought on behalf of the decedent's estate.

There are six types of damages that may be awarded in a wrongful death case. They are listed below:

Loss of love, affection, companionship, care, protection and guidance. These damages are commonly referred to as *loss of consortium* damages, and are largely discretionary.

Pain, grief, sorrow, anguish, stress, shock, and mental suffering experienced by the survivors. The survivors may recover damages for their pain and suffering, but except in an action for elder abuse, the survivors may not recover damages for the *decedent's* pain and suffering.

Loss of income and services. The survivors may recover damages for their economic loss caused by the death. The measure of these damages is the loss of economic support that each beneficiary would have received from the decedent. In cases where the wrongful death action is brought on behalf of the estate, future earnings of the decedent can be used as the measure of damages.

Funeral and burial expenses. These expenses are recoverable if the beneficiary paid them or is liable for payment.

Medical expenses. Similar to funeral and burial expenses, discussed above, these damages are recoverable only if the beneficiary paid them or is liable for payment.

Punitive damages. Punitive damages, which are intended to punish the wrongdoer, are recoverable if the person causing the death acted with an "evil mind." Punitive damages may be awarded in certain cases involving drunk drivers. The jury will determine the amount of punitive damages depending on the aggravating circumstances attending the wrongful act, neglect or default.

Legal Tips:

- A wrongful death action must be filed within two years of the death, or it will be forever barred by the statute of limitations. In some cases, especially those involving claims against government agencies or public employees, claims must be presented in a much shorter time period.
- Liability for wrongful death likely will be covered under an auto or homeowners policy of insurance.
- A person against whom a claim for wrongful death is made should immediately notify his insurance company and cooperate fully in the defense of the claim.

67

Defective and Dangerous Products

From cars to cigarettes, products cause injuries.

This body of law is commonly referred to as products liability. The manufacturer or seller of a defective and unreasonably dangerous product is liable to anyone who is injured by the proper use of the product. The theory of products liability has been asserted with success against numerous companies whose products have been found to be defective and unreasonably dangerous. In Arizona, a food product that is otherwise fit for human consumption and nourishment is not, by legal definition, "defective and unreasonably dangerous."

A product can be defective and unreasonably dangerous if it contains a manufacturing defect, a design defect, or does not come with adequate warnings or instructions.[3] Each type of defect is discussed below, with examples provided.

Manufacturing Defect

A product is defective and unreasonably dangerous because of a *manufacturing defect* if it contains a condition which the manufacturer did not intend and, as a result, it fails to perform as safely as an ordinary consumer would expect when the product is used in a reasonably foreseeable manner. Example: A lawnmower that loses a blade during normal operations, because the blades were improperly assembled during the manufacturing process.

Design Defect

A product is defective and unreasonably dangerous because of a *design defect* if the harmful characteristics or consequences of its design outweigh the benefits of the design. A product is also defective and unreasonably dangerous because of a design defect if it fails to perform as safely as an ordinary consumer would expect when the product is used in a reasonably foreseeable manner. Example: A car that bursts into flames during a rear-end collision because of the location and design of the gas tank.

Failure to Warn

A product, even if faultlessly made, is defective and unreasonably dangerous if it would be unreasonably dangerous for use in a reasonably foreseeable manner without adequate *warnings or instructions*. Example: A space heater sold without a warning that it should not be placed close to combustible materials during use.

Who is Liable?

The defective products laws apply to the "manufacturers" and "sellers" of products. These terms are broadly defined. A "manufacturer" is a person or company who designs, assembles, fabricates, produces, constructs, or otherwise prepares a product or component part of a product prior to its sale to a user or consumer. A "seller" is a person or company who is engaged in the business of leasing any product or selling any product for resale, use or consumption. The definition of seller includes wholesalers, distributors, retailers and lessors.

Before a manufacturer or seller can be found at fault, it must be determined that the product manufactured or sold was defective and unreasonably dangerous, and that the defect was a cause of the person's injury. A defect causes an injury if it helps produce the injury, and if the injury would not have happened without the defect.

A manufacturer or seller of a defective and unreasonably dangerous product must compensate the person injured by the product for his damages. In deciding damages, a jury will consider the nature, extent and duration of the injury, pain and suffering experienced, disability and disfigurement, medical expenses, and lost earnings. The spouse of the injured person may have a claim for loss of love, care, affection, companionship, and other pleasures of the marital relationship, known as a loss of consortium claim.

Statute of Limitations

A lawsuit for product liability must be filed within two years from the date on which the cause of action accrues. Generally, a cause of action will accrue on the date that the product causes injury.

68

Property Owners' Liability (Premises Liability)

"A man's home is his castle." —Proverb

This chapter deals with the liability of a property owner for injuries occurring on his property. This area of the law is commonly referred to as premises liability. It includes store premises, school property, recreational lands, and private residences.

The rule in Arizona is that the degree of care owed by a property owner depends on the legal status of the person who comes onto the land. The person who comes onto the land may be categorized as a trespasser, a licensee, or an invitee. A different degree of care is owed with respect to each type of visitor. Here are the definitions:

Trespasser: someone who enters upon land without the owner's consent or right to do so. A burglar is a trespasser.

Licensee: someone who comes upon the land for his own pleasure or convenience with the consent of the owner. A social guest is a licensee.

Invitee: someone who is invited to enter for a purpose connected with the business dealings of the owner. A grocery shopper is an invitee.

Trespassers (Intruders)

Not surprisingly, a trespasser is owed the lowest degree of care. The property owner owes a limited duty to neither willfully nor intentionally inflict an injury upon trespassers. Thus, an injured trespasser may not recover unless the property owner has been guilty of some willful or wanton disregard for his safety.

There are certain exceptions to this limited liability rule, however. A property owner may be liable for maintaining a highly dangerous artificial condition (*e.g.*, unmarked barbed wire) on his land, or if he knows or should know that trespassers constantly intrude on his land and he carries on a dangerous activity (*e.g.*, excavation), or if harm is caused by artificial conditions to trespassing *children*. (This last exception to the limited liability of landowners is known as the "attractive nuisance doctrine.")

Licensees (Social Guests)

A licensee is owed the next highest degree of protection from the property owner. A property owner is liable for injury to a licensee if caused by a hazardous condition and: 1) the owner knew or should have known of the condition; 2) the owner should have realized that the condition posed an unreasonable risk of harm; 3) the owner should have expected that the licensee would not discover or appreciate the danger; 4) the owner failed to take reasonable care to either correct the condition or warn about it; and 5) the licensee neither knew nor had reason to know of the condition and the risk. If all five of these conditions are met, the owner is liable for the licensee's injuries.

Invitees (Customers)

An invitee is owed the highest degree of protection from the property owner. Unlike the duty owed to a licensee, the owner must protect the invitee from unreasonably dangerous conditions, either known to the owner or discoverable by the exercise of reasonable care. This means that the landowner has a duty of inspection—to ensure that the land is safe for his invitees. The law is clear, however, that property owners are not required to render their premises absolutely safe.

Most slip-and-fall cases involve invitees. A store owner can be held liable to a shopper who suffers a slip and fall caused by an unreasonably dangerous condition if the owner either created the condition or had notice of it. Many dangerous conditions, such as the proverbial banana peel on the floor, are caused by other shoppers. In such cases, the store owner may be liable if the condition existed for such a length of time that in the exercise of ordinary care the store owner should have known of it and taken action to remedy it. This is why many grocery stores routinely inspect their floors and record the inspection times.

Measure of Damages

If the property owner is liable for an injury on his property, the injured person is entitled to the amount of money that will reasonably and fairly compensate him or her for the following elements of damages that resulted from the property owner's fault:

- The nature, extent, and duration of the injury.
- The pain, discomfort, suffering, disability, disfigurement, and anxiety experienced as a result of the injury.
- Reasonable and necessary medical expenses.
- Loss of earnings.
- Loss of love, care, affection, companionship, and other pleasures of the marital or family relationship.

Legal Tip:

A property owner should always maintain sufficient premises liability insurance to protect against liability for injury to visitors. A homeowner's policy will include this coverage for the home; a business policy will contain this coverage for business premises.

69

Dog Bites

"The dog, to gain some private ends, went mad and bit the man." —Oliver Goldsmith

Pet ownership is on the rise. It is estimated that there are now 75 million dogs in the United States. Every year, unfortunately, our "best friends" bite more than 4,000,000 people, most of whom are children. One out of every six dog bites is serious enough to require medical attention.

Not surprisingly, the most common lawsuit involving animals is for injuries caused by dog bites. In Arizona, the Legislature has enacted strict liability statutes covering dog bites. Additionally, a separate common-law negligence claim may be asserted against the owner of a dog with dangerous propensities.[4] We will look at each basis for liability.

Statutory Claims

One statutory provision renders the dog owner or caretaker fully responsible for damages to any person or property caused by a dog while at large. Another provision states that the owner of a dog which bites a person is liable for damages suffered by the person bitten, *regardless of the former viciousness of the dog or the owner's knowledge of its viciousness,* when the victim is: 1) in or on a public place, or 2) lawfully in or on a private place, including the property of the owner of the dog. These statutes impose strict liability on the dog owner, because they make the owner liable for damages regardless of the owner's negligence.

Proof of provocation of the attack by the person injured is the only defense to a statutory action for damages. The issue of provocation is determined by whether a *reasonable person* would expect that the conduct or circumstances would be likely to provoke a dog.

Illustration: A groomer, bitten by a dog while working at a pet hospital, was "lawfully in or on a private place" when he was bitten, and therefore, absent provocation, the owner was liable for the dog bite under the statute imposing strict liability on the owner regardless of fault.

A person is "lawfully in or on" the private property of the owner of a dog when there as an invitee or guest. The statute does not impose liability for injuries to a trespasser caused by a dog.

Negligence Claims

A separate common-law negligence claim may be asserted based on the owner's knowledge of the dog's dangerous propensities. Under this theory of liability, the owner is liable regardless of his exercise of care if he knew, or should have known, of the dog's dangerous tendencies. The dog bite victim must prove, however, that the owner knew or had reason to know of such characteristics. This proof is not required for a statutory claim, as discussed above. Punitive damages may be recovered based on a history of the dog's viciousness and the owner's inaction.

Limitation Periods

If a common-law negligence claim is more difficult to prove than a strict-liability statutory claim (which does *not* require evidence of the owner's negligence), why would anyone bring a negligence claim? The answer may lie in the time deadlines to assert the claims. The statutory claim must be brought within one year, but the negligence claim can be brought within two years. In this respect, the negligence claim has an advantage over the statutory claim. (Note: if the victim is a minor, the time does not start running until he or she turns 18.)

Animal Bite Reporting

Each county has an enforcement agent. Whenever an animal bites any person, by law the incident must be reported to the county enforcement agent immediately by any person having direct knowledge. In Maricopa County, a dog bite may be reported to Maricopa County Animal Care and Control, by calling (602) 506-7387.

All dogs that have bitten are required by law to be quarantined for 10 days. Dogs that are under quarantine are monitored for rabies. A dog that is properly vaccinated and licensed at the time of the bite may be quarantined in the owner's home.

If a dog bite victim believes that the dog is a serious threat, he can file a vicious dog petition with the city or justice court. The law defines a vicious animal as one that has a propensity to attack, to cause injury to or to otherwise endanger the safety of human beings without provocation. If the judge determines, after a hearing, that the dog is vicious, the judge may place restrictions on the dog's release—such as that the dog wear a muzzle in public— or the judge may order that the dog be destroyed.

70

Insurance Company Bad Faith

"An insurance company must give as much consideration to its insured's interests as it does to its own."

Most adults have multiple insurance policies. It is not unusual for a person to simultaneously have car insurance, homeowner's insurance, health insurance, life insurance, and title insurance. When an insurance company fails to act in good faith and deal fairly with its customers, it is guilty of bad faith. The insurance customer, or insured, may in those cases bring suit against the insurance company for bad faith.

There is an implied duty of good faith and fair dealing in every insurance policy. This legal duty is not written in the insurance policy, but exists by law. To prove that an insurance company breached the duty of good faith and fair dealing, the insured must prove: 1) that the company intentionally denied the claim, failed to pay the claim, or delayed payment of the claim without a reasonable basis; and 2) the company knew that it acted without a reasonable basis, or failed to perform an investigation to determine whether its action was supported by a reasonable basis.

An insurance company's conduct is not intentional if it is inadvertent or due to a good faith mistake. In all aspects of investigating or evaluating a claim, an insurance company is required to give as much consideration to its insured's interests as it does to its own interests.

If an insurance company acts in bad faith, the insured may be entitled to recover the following damages:

- The unpaid benefits of the policy.
- Monetary loss or damage to the insured's credit reputation.
- Emotional distress, humiliation, inconvenience, and anxiety experienced by the insured.
- Physical injury suffered by the insured.

To recover these damages, the insured must show that they resulted from the insurance company's bad faith. The jury or the court will decide the amount of money that will reasonably and fairly compensate the insured for his damages.

71

Negligent Misrepresentation

"Now what I want is facts...Facts alone are wanted in life."
—Charles Dickens

Negligent misrepresentation is a tort. This tort may be asserted against a person who supplies false or incorrect information in the course of his business, profession, or employment, or in a transaction in which he has a monetary interest.

A person claiming negligent misrepresentation (the "plaintiff") must prove all of the following: 1) the person being sued (the "defendant") either provided the plaintiff with false or incorrect information, or omitted or failed to disclose material information; 2) the defendant intended that the plaintiff rely on the information provided and provided it for that purpose; 3) the defendant failed to exercise reasonable care or competence in obtaining or communicating the information; 4) the plaintiff relied on the information; 5) the plaintiff's reliance was justified; and 6) as a result, the plaintiff was damaged. There is no requirement that the plaintiff prove the defendant was lying, so long as the information provided by the defendant was false.

The Arizona Supreme Court has said that "liability for negligent misrepresentation is narrow in scope because it is premised on the reasonable expectations of a foreseeable user of information supplied in connection with commercial transactions." (The author has seen the tort of negligent misrepresentation asserted against real estate agents and business promoters, who supplied false information in their transactions.)

A person who has been injured or damaged because he justifiably relied on incorrect information in a commercial transaction is entitled to reasonable compensation. As with other torts, the amount of compensation generally will be determined by a jury or judge.

A lawsuit for negligent misrepresentation must be filed within two years from when the cause of action accrues, or it will be barred by the statute of limitations.

72

Fraud

"A liar is worse than a thief." —Proverb

A person who intentionally lies to another person about a matter of importance may be guilty of fraud. The person who has been defrauded may, in addition to pressing criminal charges, file a tort claim for damages. If successful, the defrauded person may recover his actual damages and, in appropriate cases, punitive damages. This chapter discusses the tort of common law fraud.

What are the differences between consumer fraud (discussed in Chapter 16) and common law fraud? First, it is easier to prove a case for consumer fraud, because less proof is required for consumer fraud than for common law fraud. Second, the time limit to file a case for consumer fraud is one year; the time limit for common law fraud is three years (see Chapter 84 for time limits to file lawsuits). Third, consumer fraud is limited to cases involving the sale or advertisement of merchandise, and common law fraud is not.

To establish a case for common law fraud, the injured party (the "plaintiff") must prove, by clear and convincing evidence,[5] that the person committing the fraud (the "defendant") knowingly made a false representation to the plaintiff concerning an important matter, with the intent that the plaintiff would act upon the misrepresentation, that the plaintiff, not knowing the representation was false, reasonably and justifiably relied on the representation, and as a result was damaged.

A person who has been defrauded may be awarded punitive damages if he can show, also by clear and convincing evidence, that the other person acted with an "evil mind." An evil mind may be shown by intent to cause injury or wrongful conduct motivated by spite or ill will. While there is no limit to the amount of punitive damages that may be awarded in a particular case, the United States Supreme Court has suggested that punitive damages of more than nine times the actual damages may be excessive.

73

Wrongful Discharge from Employment

Wrongful discharge is wrong.

Wrongful discharge means that an employee's discharge violates the terms of his employment agreement or is against public policy. If an employee is wrongfully discharged, he is entitled to recover damages against his former employer, either for breach of contract or for the public policy tort claim. This chapter analyzes both types of wrongful discharge claims.

Breach of Employment Agreement

In Arizona, the law presumes that employment is "at will." This means that an employer may discharge an employee for *any* reason or for no reason at all, but may not discharge an employee for an unlawful reason.

Every employment agreement contains a duty to act fairly and in good faith. This duty is implied by law and has the same force and effect as if it were set forth in writing. This duty requires that neither party do anything that prevents the other from receiving the benefits of the agreement. If the employer breaches the duty of good faith and fair dealing, the employee will be entitled to recover as damages those benefits of the agreement that were denied.

An employee, to establish a breach of an employment agreement, must prove: 1) that there was an agreement between him and the employer that changed their "at will" relationship; 2) the specific terms of the agreement; 3) that the employer breached the agreement; and 4) the damages suffered by him.

If the employer breaches an employment agreement, the employee will be entitled to an amount of money that reasonably and fairly compensates him for that breach. The damage award is designed to, as nearly as possible, put the employee in the same monetary position that he would have been in had the employer not breached the agreement. That amount will be the value of all sums that would have been due from the time of the breach through the end of the agreement, less any sums that reasonably could have been or, in fact, were earned from substitute employment before the end of the agreement.

A terminated employee has a duty to make reasonable efforts to reduce damages by trying to find substantially similar employment. He has no responsibility to accept employment that is not substantially similar to his prior employment, nor does he have a responsibility to accept employment that imposes an undue burden or hardship. If a terminated employee could have reduced damages but failed to do so, then his award will be reduced by the amount of damages that he could have reasonably avoided.

Illustration: A pastry chef is wrongfully terminated from his job at a four-star restaurant. He is then offered a job to make fancy desserts for a catering company, but declines the employment. He receives no other job offers. Because he refused to accept substantially similar employment, his award will be reduced by the amounts that he could have earned by working for the catering company before the end of the agreement with his former employer.

Public Policy Tort Claim

As mentioned above, an employer may not discharge an employee for a reason that violates public policy. If the employer does so, that employee has been wrongfully discharged and may bring a public policy tort claim against his former employer. An employer will have violated Arizona's public policy by discharging an employee:

- because of discrimination based on race, color, religion, sex, age, disability or national origin, or
- in retaliation for filing a complaint of discrimination, or
- in retaliation for refusing to engage in unlawful conduct, or
- in retaliation for exercising a legal right, or
- in retaliation for "whistleblowing" because he reported or attempted to report illegal or unsafe acts of the employer.

The law protects the act of reporting discrimination or whistleblowing, even if it is later determined that there was no discrimination or the conduct that he reported was not illegal or unsafe. The discharged employee must, however, show that he had a good faith belief that what was being reported constituted discrimination or an illegal or unsafe practice.

If an employer discharges an employee in violation of Arizona's public policy, the discharged employee will be entitled to money to compensate him for his lost earnings, mental anguish and emotional distress, physical injury, harm to his reputation, and lost insurance coverage for his medical bills.

Legal Tip:

It may be necessary to file a charge with the Equal Employment Opportunity Commission or the Arizona Civil Rights Division before filing a lawsuit against an employer for certain public policy tort claims. Please refer to the next chapter for information on filing a charge of employment discrimination in Arizona.

74

Sexual Harassment

"The law condemns sexual harassment as a matter of public policy."

Sexual harassment is illegal. A person who is sexually harassed in Arizona may file a charge against her employer with the U.S. Equal Employment Opportunity Commission (EEOC) or the Arizona Civil Rights Division, and then, if appropriate, sue her employer for sexual harassment.

This chapter provides the basic information necessary for an employee to make a claim for sexual harassment. (In so doing, it also provides the basic information necessary for an employer *to avoid* a charge of sexual harassment.)

Filing a Charge of Employment Discrimination

A person who has been sexually harassed may file a charge against her employer with the EEOC. In Arizona, the charge must be filed with the Phoenix District Office of the EEOC, located at 3300 North Central Avenue, Suite 690, Phoenix, Arizona 85012-9688. A person with an employment discrimination claim or wishing to file a charge may call the EEOC National Contact Center toll-free at 1-800-669-4000 or 1-800-669-6820 (TTY).

A person usually has 300 days from the date of the harm to file a charge with the EEOC against an employer with *15 or more employees* (for discrimination in Arizona based on sex). Charges against employers of *less than 15 employees* for discrimination based on sex must be filed with the Arizona Civil Rights Division within 180 days. The Arizona Civil Rights Division may be contacted by calling (602) 542-5263 (Phoenix) or (520) 628-6500 (Tucson), or through its website: www.ag.state.az.us.

A charge of discrimination will be investigated by the agency with which it is filed. If a charge cannot be resolved by the agency, then the person filing the charge may file a lawsuit against her employer for sexual harassment.

Lawsuit for Sexual Harassment

A sexual harassment lawsuit will generally be filed in the superior court of the county in which the harassment occurred. The employee will be the plaintiff, and the employer will be the defendant in the case.

To establish this claim, the employee must prove that she was sexually harassed *and* that she was damaged as a result of the harassment.

Sexual harassment occurs when a supervisor expressly or impliedly makes unwelcome sexual conduct as a condition of the plaintiff's employment or the receipt of job benefits, or both.

A hostile work environment may also constitute sexual harassment. This occurs when: 1) a supervisor, co-employee, or other person makes sexual advances, requests for sexual conduct, or engages in other verbal or physical conduct of a sexual nature, which a reasonable person would find offensive; 2) the conduct was unwelcome; and 3) the conduct was sufficiently severe or widespread to alter the condition of the plaintiff's employment and create an abusive working environment. If the employer knew or should have known of the hostile work environment and failed to take appropriate action, then the employer is liable for sexual harassment.

If an employer is found to have sexually harassed an employee, the harassed employee will be entitled to money to compensate her for her lost earnings, mental anguish and emotional distress, physical injury, harm to her reputation, and lost insurance coverage for her medical bills.

Legal Tip:

A person, to protect his or her legal rights, should contact the EEOC or Arizona Civil Rights Division promptly when discrimination is suspected. The time limits for filing a charge for discrimination are strictly enforced.

75

Breach of Contract

In civil courts, more cases are filed for breach of contract than any other.

About one-third of all civil lawsuits filed in Arizona are for breach of contract. That translates into more than 35,000 new breach of contract cases every year in the state of Arizona. This chapter looks at breach of contract claims in Arizona.

The Basics

What is a contract? A contract is simply an agreement between two or more persons. It may be written or oral. It may also, under appropriate circumstances, be implied by law.

For a contract to legally exist there must be an offer, acceptance of the offer, and either a benefit received or something given up or exchanged, known as "consideration." There is no contract if there is no consideration. Failure of consideration occurs when a party fails to do something required by the contract which is so important to the contract that the failure defeats the very purpose of the contract.

Illustration: Fred offers to sell his used car to Barney for $1,000. Barney accepts Fred's offer, but fails to pay the agreed price. There is no consideration for the contract, and Fred will be excused from performance. Thus, Fred will be free to sell his car to someone else.

"Substantial Performance" of a Contract

In some cases, especially in the field of construction, one party may claim that the other party did not fully complete the contract. (In construction cases, this is referred to as "substantial completion.") The party making that claim probably is trying to avoid payment. If a party has substantially performed, then he is entitled to payment from the other party.

Substantial performance means that a party has performed all that is required by the contract, except for slight defects that can be easily cured. To determine whether a party has substantially performed his obligations under a contract, consideration will be given to the nature of the promised performance, the purpose of the contract, and the extent to which any defects in performance have defeated that purpose. Returning to the construction area, if there has been substantial although not full performance, the building contractor will have a claim for the unpaid balance and the owner will have a claim only for damages.

Contract Conditions

A contract will not be enforced where its performance depends on an event (condition) not certain to occur, and that event does not occur. This is known as failure of condition. A condition may be *waived* by a party, if the condition is intended solely for that party's benefit.

A party to a contract may also waive what the other party agreed to do as his part of the contract. Waiver is an intentional relinquishment of a known right. ("I waive my right to payment.") A waiver may be expressly stated by a party, or it may be implied by or inferred from actions taken by him. By knowingly and unconditionally accepting defective performance, a party will have waived any objection to it. If a party waives a promised performance, then the other party is no longer bound to perform on that promise.

Intent not to Perform Contract

If one party states or shows his intent not to perform a contract as promised, and the other party is ready, willing and offers to perform his duties under the contract, the first party will be guilty of anticipatory breach. This means that the party who conveyed his intent not to perform will be liable to the other party for *breach* of contract.

Claims by Contract Beneficiaries

A person who is not a party to a contract may sometimes sue for breach of contract, as a "third-party beneficiary." To prove this claim, the third party must show that: 1) the parties intended that he directly benefit from the contract; 2) the parties intended to recognize him as the primary party in interest; and 3) the contract itself indicated an intent to benefit him or a class of persons including him. (A beneficiary named in a life insurance policy is a good example of a third-party beneficiary.)

Duty of Good Faith and Fair Dealing

Every party to a contract, whether oral or written, has a duty to act fairly and in good faith. This duty is implied by law and need not be in writing.

This duty requires that neither party do anything that prevents the other party from receiving the benefits of their agreement. If a party breaches the duty of good faith and fair dealing, the other party will be entitled to recover any damages that resulted from the breach.

"Direct Damages" for Breach of Contract

If a party breaches a contract, he will be required to compensate the other party for all damages that resulted *naturally and directly* from the breach of contract. The damages will be the amount of money that will place the nonbreaching party in the position he would have been in if the contract had been performed. To determine those direct damages, consideration will be given to: 1) the profit that the nonbreaching party would have received had the contract been performed; 2) the return of the value of the things or services that he provided to the other party; or 3) the value of things or services expended by him in preparing to perform his part of the contract or in preparing to accept the benefits of the other party's expected performance. Consideration will also be given to whether the party, by not having to perform his part of the contract, avoided any cost or loss which should be deducted from his damages.

The nonbreaching party must prove his damages in a breach of contract case with specific evidence. Ordinarily, a party may recover on only one of the three damage elements stated in the preceding paragraph; the law will not allow double recovery of damages under more than one theory.

"Consequential Damages" for Breach of Contract

A party may recover both direct and consequential damages. Direct damages are those which, in the ordinary course of human experience, can be expected to result directly from a breach (see above discussion). *Consequential damages* do not flow directly from a breach, but arise because of special circumstances. To recover for consequential damages, a party must show: 1) that it was foreseeable to the parties when they entered into the contract that these damages would probably result if the contract was breached; 2) that these damages were in fact caused by the other party's breach of contract; and 3) the amount of the damages.

Lost Profits

To recover damages for lost profits, a party must show: 1) that it is reasonably probable that the profits would have been earned except for the breach; 2) that the loss of profits is the direct and natural consequence of the breach; and 3) the amount of lost profits can be shown with reasonable certainty. The amount of lost profits cannot be based on conjecture or speculation. In determining lost profits, it is appropriate to subtract the costs and expenses the party would have incurred from the gross revenue he would have received if the contract had not been breached.

Duty to Reduce Damages

A party may not recover for any damages that could have been prevented or reduced through reasonable efforts. The party objecting to damages must prove: 1) that the party claiming damages did not make reasonable efforts to prevent or reduce damages; 2) that if the party claiming damages had acted reasonably, he could have prevented or reduced damages; and 3) the amount of damages that could have been prevented or reduced through reasonable efforts.

Award of Attorney's Fees and Costs

A person who wins a lawsuit arising out of a contract, either express or implied, may be entitled to an award of his reasonable attorney's fees. To recover attorney's fees, the successful party will be required to submit a detailed application for attorney's fees to the judge at the end of the case. The judge has the authority in contract cases to award fees to the successful party, and will generally do so. In some cases (sad to say), the attorney's fees can be even more than the amount of contract damages. The successful party will also be entitled to award of his court costs.

Author's Note:

In the law, there are literally more reported contract cases than can be counted (at least by this author). First-year law students are required to take (and pass) a course on contract law, and in that class they spend countless hours studying and debating contract issues and cases.

It is, therefore, unreasonable to assume that a fair treatment of the subject has been rendered in this short chapter. At best, it is hoped that this chapter has achieved its intended purpose—to provide a fair overview of the subject—and that the reader will consult an attorney if a contract issue arises.

76

Interference With Contract

A man may not interfere with another's contract.

A contract is an agreement between two or more people. It may be written or oral. If a third party interferes with a contract, the third party may be liable for money damages resulting from his interference.

This claim is known as interference with contract. To establish this claim, the injured person (the "plaintiff") must show: 1) that he had a contract with another person; 2) that a third person (the "defendant") knew about the contract; 3) that the defendant intentionally interfered with the plaintiff's contractual relationship with the other person, which caused a breach or termination of that relationship; 4) that the defendant's conduct was improper; and 5) that the plaintiff suffered damages caused by the breach or termination of the plaintiff's contractual relationship with the other person.

This claim is available to any person who suffers a loss as a result of another person's improper interference with his contractual relationship, regardless of the subject matter of the contract. In the area of employment law, this claim may be asserted by an employee against a third person who improperly interferes with his employment agreement. It may also be asserted by an employer against a third person who improperly interferes with an agreement between the employer and an employee.

If a person improperly interferes with another person's contract, then the wrongdoer will have to pay money damages to the injured person (*i.e.*, the plaintiff). These damages will consist of the net profit or benefit that the plaintiff would have received had the contract been performed, damage to the plaintiff's reputation, and any emotional suffering sustained by the plaintiff. A judge or jury will determine the amount of the damages, based on the facts of the case.

The time limit to file a lawsuit for interference with contract is two years from when the cause of action accrues.

77

Payment for Services Without a Contract (Implied Contracts)

"It is the nature of men to be bound by the benefits they confer as much as by those they receive." — Machiavelli

When a person is employed in the services of another for any period of time, the law implies a promise to pay what the services are reasonably worth. The name for this legal theory is *quantum meruit*. It applies in cases where there is no express contract between the parties.

A person is entitled to recover the reasonable value of the services rendered by him, unless it was understood by the parties that the services were being rendered free of charge, or unless it was not unfair for the party receiving the benefit of the services to not pay for them. Two illustrations:

Illustration #1: Two neighbors agree to share the cost of constructing a block wall on their common property line. One neighbor, who happens to be a mason, builds the wall and the two neighbors equally share the cost of the work. The wall is later severely damaged when a tree falls on it during a storm. The mason, with his neighbor's knowledge, proceeds to repair the wall. Under these circumstances, it would be unfair to allow the one neighbor to retain the benefit of the work without paying for it. He will be required to pay for his share of the work.

Illustration #2: One neighbor, while another neighbor is

away, washes a car left in the absent neighbor's driveway. It rains before the neighbor returns home. Under these circumstances, no payment for the voluntary car wash is required.

In awarding a person the reasonable value of his services under this legal theory, the nature of the services provided and the customary rate of pay for the services will be considered. The award will include the value of both labor and materials furnished.

78

Breach of Fiduciary Duties

"A fiduciary relationship exists whenever one party trusts and relies upon another party." —Texas Court of Appeals

A fiduciary is a person who has a relationship with another based generally on trust and confidence. Escrow agents, trustees, attorneys and partners are all examples of fiduciaries. (A fiduciary may also be a company, such as a title company, bank or trust company.)

A fiduciary owes a special duty to the other person in the relationship. This is called a "fiduciary duty." If a fiduciary breaches this duty, the injured person may sue the fiduciary for breach of fiduciary duty. In this chapter, we will look at some fiduciary relationships and duties.

Escrow Agents

An escrow agent is usually employed by the buyer and seller in a real estate transaction, to handle the escrow pending the close of the transaction. An escrow agent is often a title company.

An escrow agent owes a fiduciary duty to the parties in a transaction. This duty requires the escrow agent to conduct the transaction with scrupulous care, honesty and diligence. It also requires the escrow agent to disclose information known to the agent that presented evidence of fraud.

Trustees

A trustee may be appointed by the court, or may be named in a trust agreement. A trustee may be an individual, or a bank or trust company. A trustee administers the property of others.

A trustee owes a fiduciary duty to the parties to a trust agreement, and to the beneficiaries of the trust being administered by the trustee. This duty requires the trustee to act as a reasonable person and, in appropriate cases, to use its special skills and expertise in dealing with the property of others.

Attorneys

Attorneys owe a fiduciary duty to their clients. This duty requires attorneys to represent clients with strictest loyalty and to act with the highest and utmost good faith.

Partners

A partnership is a legal entity consisting of two or more partners. Partners owe a fiduciary duty to one another. This duty requires partners to deal in utmost good faith with one another and to fully disclose to one another all material facts relating to partnership affairs within their knowledge. In the case of a limited partnership, the general partner owes this duty to the limited partners.

Before a person can be found liable for breach of fiduciary duty, it must be shown that his breach of duty was a cause of the other person's damages. A breach of duty is a cause of damages if it helps produce the damages and if the damages would not have occurred without the breach.

A breach of fiduciary duty is a tort. A fiduciary who is found liable for breach of fiduciary duty will be required to pay for all damages that occurred as a result of the breach. In a trial, the amount of damages will be determined by the judge or a jury.

The time limit to file a lawsuit for breach of fiduciary duty is two years from when the cause of action accrues.

79

Liability for Recording False Documents

"True and false are attributes of speech, not of things."
—Thomas Hobbes

A false document is one that is forged, groundless, contains a material misstatement or false claim, or is otherwise invalid. The recording of a false document with the county recorder[6] will subject the person to both civil and criminal liability under Arizona's false documents statute.

Civil Liability

The county recorder generally will accept for recording any document that is presented in recordable form. The county recorder does *not* verify the validity of a document presented to him for recording. Deeds, deeds of trust, mortgages, and mechanic's liens are typical of the documents recorded in the office of the county recorder.

A person claiming an interest in, or a lien or encumbrance against real property, who causes a document asserting the claim to be recorded in the office of the county recorder, knowing or having reason to know that the document is false (as defined above), is liable to the owner of the property for damages. The property owner will be entitled to recover $5,000 or three times the actual damages caused by the recording, whichever is greater, plus the owner's reasonable attorney's fees and court costs.

A person who is named in a document which attempts to create an interest in, or a lien or encumbrance against real property, and who knows the document is false, must release or correct the document within 20 days from the date of a written request from the owner to do so. If the person refuses to release or correct the document, he will be liable to the owner for $1,000 or for three times actual damages, whichever is greater, plus attorney's fees and costs.

The owner of the property may file a lawsuit pursuant to the false documents statute in the superior court in the county in which the property is located. In addition to recovering damages, the owner may obtain a court order that clears title to his property.

A lawsuit for false document recording must be filed within one year from when the cause of action accrues, or it will be barred by the statute of limitations. A beneficial title holder has all of the same rights and remedies as the owner under the statute.

Criminal Liability

The recording of a false document could also subject the person to jail time and/or a fine. A person who records any document claiming an interest in, or a lien or encumbrance against real property, when he knows that the document is forged, contains a material misstatement or false claim, or is otherwise invalid, is guilty of a class 1 misdemeanor. This crime is seldom prosecuted, however.

80

Liability of Persons Selling or Serving Alcohol

Arizona's Dramshop Act

It is illegal for a person to manufacture, sell or deal in spirituous liquors in Arizona without being properly licensed. A person to whom a liquor license is issued is called a "licensee." The law imposes civil liability on a licensee who serves an intoxicated person or a person under 21 years of age who, in turn, causes property damage, personal injuries or death.

A licensee may be liable for property damage and personal injuries, or to a person who may bring an action for wrongful death, if the licensee sold alcohol either to someone who was *obviously intoxicated*, or to an underage drinker without requesting proper identification or with knowledge that the person was under 21. For the licensee to be liable, the purchaser must consume the alcohol sold by the licensee and the consumption must be the proximate cause of the injury, death or property damage.

The term "obviously intoxicated" means inebriated to such an extent that a person's physical faculties are substantially impaired and the impairment is shown by significantly uncoordinated physical action or significant physical dysfunction, that would have been obvious to a reasonable person.

If an underage person purchases alcohol from a licensee and that person incurs or causes injuries or property damage as a result of the consumption of alcohol within a reasonable period of time following the sale of the alcohol, it will be presumed that the underage person consumed the alcohol sold by the licensee.

A licensee is *not* liable to any consumer or purchaser of alcohol over the legal drinking age who is injured or whose property is damaged as a result of the sale or serving of alcohol to that person. Similarly, a licensee is not liable in damages to any other adult who was with the person when the alcohol was drank and who knew of the impaired condition of the person.

The law contains a social host exemption. A social host is not liable to any person who is injured, or to the survivors of any person killed, or for damage to property, which is caused by the furnishing or serving of alcohol to a person of legal drinking age. However, this exemption does not apply to a social host who furnishes alcohol to an underage drinker.

81

Injury to Child

First, protect the children.

A child may be injured by another person's careless, reckless or intentional acts. In those cases, the child's parents or guardian may bring suit against the person or persons responsible for the child's injuries. The child is not a proper party in a lawsuit to recover damages for his or her injuries.

If a child has a guardian, the guardian may sue or defend in court on behalf of the child (please refer to Chapter 58 for information about a guardian's legal rights and duties). If a child does not have a guardian or other fiduciary, the child may sue by a next friend or a guardian *ad litem*.[7] A child's mother or father may serve as the child's next friend or guardian *ad litem*, subject to approval by the court.

The court will appoint a guardian *ad litem* for a child not otherwise represented in a lawsuit, or will make another order as it deems proper for the protection of the child.

If an action is brought for a minor by a next friend or guardian *ad litem*, the friend or guardian may not receive any money or property of the child until he or she files a surety bond with the court, as security for the faithful performance of his or her duties.

A next friend or guardian will not be personally liable for costs of the suit, unless by special order of the court. The court may allow the next friend or guardian a reasonable compensation for his or her services.

The time limits for filing suit do not begin to run until the minor reaches 18 years of age. At that time, the person who suffered injuries as a minor may file suit in his or her own name, as an adult. However, because evidence spoils, memories fade, and witnesses move (or die) over time, it is often wise to file suit on behalf of a minor as soon as possible after the injury-causing event.

82

Justice Courts and Small Claims

Using Arizona's lower courts

Civil lawsuits involving $10,000 or less can be processed relatively inexpensively and quickly in Arizona's justice of the peace courts ("justice courts"). This chapter contains information on justice courts and small claims in Arizona.

Arizona's Justice Courts

Every county in Arizona has at least two justice courts. The justice courts have exclusive authority to hear cases in which the amount in controversy is $10,000 or less.[8] Cases in which the amount in controversy is greater than $10,000 must be filed in the superior court.

If a defendant files a counterclaim in justice court for more than $10,000, the case will be immediately transferred to the superior court.

An action should be filed in the justice court located where the person or company being sued resides or does business, or where the cause of action occurred. Location information for all of the justice courts in Arizona may be obtained from the Arizona Supreme Court's Web site, www.azcourts.gov/azcourts/azcourtslocator.aspx.

The rules of procedure for the superior courts are followed in justice courts, but fewer of the courtroom formalities are observed. Many people choose to represent themselves in justice court, because the system is fairly user-friendly. The justice court clerks generally furnish, free of charge, all of the forms needed in a civil case. (In Maricopa County, court information and forms are available online, at www.superiorcourt.maricopa.gov/justicecourts/index.asp.)

Because civil cases are processed quicker in justice courts than in superior court, it takes less time to obtain a final determination. This means that the parties spend less time and money in court. It also means quicker collection of amounts owed.

Small Claims

Every justice court in Arizona has a small claims division to provide an even more inexpensive and speedy method for resolving civil disputes involving no more than $2,500. The small claims division is available to any person or company who wishes to file a small claims action. Lawyers are not allowed to participate in a small claims case, unless all of the parties agree, or unless they are representing themselves.

Any party may object to the proceedings being held in the small claims division. The case will then be transferred out of the small claims division. Once the case is transferred, the small claims rules (see next paragraph) no longer apply.

All cases in the small claims division are heard by either a judge or hearing officer, who makes a decision. The decision is final and binding on both parties. There is no right to a jury trial or an appeal in a small claims case. The formal rules of procedure do not apply. The procedures in small claims cases are intended to be simple enough for a person to file all of the necessary forms and represent himself at an informal hearing. The hearing will be scheduled within 60 days from the date the defendant files an answer with the court (about 83 days from when the complaint is filed).

Legal Tip:

If you have a claim involving $10,000 or less, consider filing it in the justice court. If the claim does not exceed $2,500, file it in the small claims division of the justice court, for an even more inexpensive and speedy resolution.

83

Mediation and Arbitration
of Disputes

"For many claims, trials by adversarial contest must in time go the way of the ancient trial by battle and blood." —Chief Justice Warren Burger, 1984

What Chief Justice Burger went on to say is that our civil justice system is too costly, too painful and too inefficient for a civilized society. In response to these problems—noted by the Chief Justice over 25 years ago—many people today choose mediation and arbitration, instead of litigation, to resolve their disputes. In this chapter, we will look at the benefits of these "alternative dispute resolution" methods.

Mediation

Mediation is a process in which a neutral person (the "mediator"), often a retired judge, assists the parties in reaching their own settlement, but the mediator does not have the authority to make a binding decision. Before becoming a mediator, a person must generally complete a minimum number of hours of mediation training.

In the superior court, the parties are required to confer early in the case about the possibilities for a prompt settlement or resolution of the case and whether they might benefit from participating in some alternative dispute resolution (ADR) process. Within 30 days after their conference, the parties must inform the judge about any ADR agreements or possibilities. The superior court and justice courts strongly encourage mediation of disputes, and many courts sponsor mediation programs.

During mediation, each party is given a chance to explain his position to the other party and to the mediator. The mediator will help the parties explore different solutions to their problems. The purpose of mediation is not to prove which party's version of the facts is true, but rather to discuss the problems and potential solutions.

A mediator will not force any party to agree to a solution against his wishes. However, if the parties voluntarily reach a settlement, the mediator will assist the parties in putting the settlement in writing. Under the court rules, a written settlement reached through mediation is binding. The parties may then submit the agreement to the judge for approval. If the parties do not reach a settlement through mediation, they may take their case to court the same as though mediation had never occurred. All statements made during mediation are confidential, and may not be used by either party against the other in court.

Arbitration

Arbitration is the submission of a dispute to one or more impartial persons for a *final and binding* decision. Arbitration may be required by the terms of a contract, or it may be ordered by the court in cases involving relatively small amounts. (For information concerning court-ordered arbitration, please refer to Chapter 60.) We will deal here with arbitration agreed to by the parties in a contract.

Arbitration clauses are typically contained in insurance policies, construction contracts, real estate contracts, sales contracts, and employment agreements. A written agreement to submit a controversy to arbitration will be enforced by the courts in Arizona. If one party to an arbitration agreement refuses to arbitrate, the other party may obtain an order from the superior court to compel arbitration. The public policy of Arizona favors the arbitration of disputes between parties.

If the arbitration agreement provides a method of appointment of arbitrators, that method will be followed. In the absence of an agreed method, the superior court judge will appoint one or more arbitrators. The power of the arbitrators will be exercised by a majority, unless otherwise provided by the agreement or by law.

Unless otherwise provided in an arbitration agreement, the arbitrators will appoint a time and place for the hearing, and so notify the parties. The parties are entitled to be heard, to present evidence, and to cross-examine witnesses appearing at the hearing. Any party has the right to be represented by an attorney at the arbitration hearing.

At the end of the arbitration hearing, the arbitrator or arbitrators will issue an award. The award may include provisions for the payment of attorney's fees and costs by one party to the other. Either party may file an application with the superior court to confirm the arbitration award. The court will confirm the award, unless it finds it was obtained by corruption, fraud, or other undue means or it is defective for some other legal reason. In extreme cases, the court may order that another arbitration be held. Once an arbitration award is confirmed, it has the same force and effect as a judgment of the court.

The American Arbitration Association (AAA) often is designated by parties entering into an arbitration agreement. The AAA has administered over two million cases since its establishment in 1926. It presently handles nearly a quarter million cases a year, and is the nation's largest ADR provider. The AAA maintains a panel of about 7,000 arbitrators and mediators worldwide, and many of them are bilingual or multilingual. It has offices in all major cities.

For additional ADR information, the reader may wish to visit the Maricopa County Superior Court's Web site, www. superiorcourt.maricopa.gov/superiorcourt/alternativedisputeresolution/index.asp, or the AAA's Web site, www.adr.org. Both are excellent sources of information.

84

Time Limits to File Lawsuits

"A person who sits on his legal rights may lose them." — Legal maxim

The law imposes time limits for the filing of lawsuits. These time limits are known as statutes of limitations. If a lawsuit is not filed before the expiration of the statute of limitations, it will be barred. This means that it may never be filed. The Arizona statutes of limitations for various actions are set forth below.

One Year – Malicious prosecution, false imprisonment, libel or slander, seduction or breach of promise to marry, breach of employment contract, wrongful termination, and liability created by statute (*e.g.*, consumer fraud, recording false documents, and bad checks).

Two Years – Personal injury, injury when death ensues (wrongful death), damage to property, conversion of property, product liability, medical malpractice, and forcible entry and detainer.

Three Years – Oral debt, stated or open accounts, and relief on grounds of fraud or mistake.

Four Years – Bond to convey realty, partnership account, account between merchants, judgment or instrument rendered or executed outside Arizona, breach of sale contract, bond of personal representative or guardian, specific performance of contract to convey realty, and any action (other than for recovery of real property) for which no limitation is otherwise prescribed.

Five Years – Renewal of judgment; failure to make return on execution.

Six Years – Written contract for debt.

A statute of limitations begins to run when the related cause of action accrues. A cause of action generally accrues when the event occurs. In some cases, the statute of limitations may be stopped (tolled) or extended.

A statute of limitations does not begin to run until a person reaches the age of 18 years. It may be extended in cases where the person being sued was absent from the state to avoid legal process, or filed bankruptcy. There are other situations in which a statute of limitations may be tolled or extended, and an attorney should always be consulted to make that determination.

Note: In cases involving the federal government, the state, a county, or any government entity or agency (whether state or federal), written notice of the claim must generally be given to the governmental party within a specified time after the claim accrues, regardless of the length of the statute of limitations. The claim periods are usually much shorter than the corresponding statutes of limitations. Failure to give written notice of a claim within the time required by law (not covered here) will prevent a lawsuit based on that claim.

The statutes of limitations set forth above do not apply to claims arising under federal law, for which separate time limits apply.

85

Renewal of Judgments

A judgment, unless renewed, expires after five years.

A judgment is a court order that usually requires the payment of money by one party to another (a person owing money under a judgment is called a judgment debtor). In Arizona, a judgment expires after five years unless it is properly renewed. This chapter discusses the procedure to renew a judgment in Arizona.[9]

A judgment for the payment of money which has been entered by the United States district court or by the superior court may be renewed by filing an affidavit for renewal with the clerk of the proper court. The affidavit may be filed within 90 days before the expiration of five years from the judgment entry date. If the renewal affidavit is filed either too early or too late, it will be invalid and the judgment will expire.

The renewal affidavit must set forth specific information concerning the judgment, including the names of the parties, recording information, the status of collection, and the amount owed on the judgment. The specific information that must be included in the renewal affidavit is set forth in the judgment renewal statute, A.R.S. Section 12-1612, the text of which may be downloaded from the Arizona State Legislature's Web site, www.azleg.gov.

The filing of a renewal affidavit in the office of the clerk of the court where the judgment was entered renews the judgment to the extent of the balance shown due in the affidavit. Additional and successive affidavits may be filed within 90 days of expiration of five years from the date of the filing of a prior renewal affidavit. Thus, a judgment may be renewed indefinitely by properly filing renewal affidavits every five years.

A judgment that is recorded in the county recorder's office constitutes a lien against any property owned by the judgment debtor in that county. A judgment may be recorded in more than one county. However, no lien on the property of the judgment debtor will be continued by an affidavit of renewal until a certified copy of the affidavit is recorded in the office of the county recorder. If the judgment has been recorded in more than one county, a certified copy of the renewal affidavit must be recorded in each such county.

Part Six

Business Law

86

Formation and Operation of Corporations

*Shareholders are not personally liable
for the debts of the corporation.*

A corporation is a form of business ownership. The owners of a corporation are called shareholders. Shareholders generally are not personally liable for the debts and liabilities of the corporation. The shareholders risk only the investment they make in the business to purchase their shares. Thus, the owners of a corporation (its shareholders) have only limited liability. It is the concept of limited liability that makes a corporation a good form of business ownership for someone starting a business who wants to shield his personal assets from the debts of his business.

Formation of a Corporation

One or more persons may form a corporation in Arizona. The persons forming the corporation are called "incorporators." The incorporators must file Articles of Incorporation and a certificate of disclosure with the Arizona Corporation Commission. The corporation commission charges a filing fee, which at the time of this writing is $60 for regular filing and $95 for expedited filing.

Articles of Incorporation

The Articles of Incorporation must include the name of the corporation, a brief statement of its initial business, the number of shares the corporation will be authorized to issue, the address of the known place of business in Arizona, and the name and address of each incorporator, initial director and the statutory agent. (The statutory agent is the person who receives legal papers for the corporation.)

The Articles of Incorporation may include other provisions "not inconsistent with law" that the incorporators may elect to set forth. In some instances, the incorporators will include provisions in the articles limiting the liability of directors for actions taken by them on behalf of the corporation.

The Articles of Incorporation must be signed by the incorporators and the statutory agent.

Certificate of Disclosure

The second document required to form a corporation— the certificate of disclosure—must state whether any person associated with the corporation has been convicted of a felony involving certain crimes within the past seven years: has been involved in the violation of securities laws, consumer fraud laws or antitrust laws within the past seven years; or has ever served in a similar capacity in another corporation that was placed in bankruptcy, receivership, or had its charter revoked. If the answer to any of these questions is "yes," additional detailed information must be provided to the corporation commission before the Article of Incorporation will be approved. The certificate of disclosure must be signed by the incorporators under penalty of perjury, and updated at least annually when the corporation files its annual report.

Organizational Meeting & Publication

After the Articles of Incorporation are filed, an organizational meeting of directors must be held for the purpose of adopting bylaws (the internal rules of the corporation), electing officers, and transacting other initial business. The corporation must also, within 60 days from the filing of the articles, publish a copy of the articles in a newspaper of general circulation in the county of the known place of business in Arizona, for three consecutive publications. Upon completion of the publication, the newspaper will provide an affidavit of publication. The affidavit must be filed with the Arizona Corporation Commission.

Operation of the Corporation

Stock

The corporation issues shares of stock to its owners. As noted above, the owners of a corporation are known as shareholders, and the shareholders have limited liability. Under Arizona law, stock may be issued in exchange for any property or benefit to the corporation, including cash or services performed. However, stock may not be issued in exchange for future services or promissory notes. The board of directors has the power to determine the amount of consideration that is adequate in exchange for shares issued by the corporation. If the corporation issues stock to the public, state and federal securities laws impose numerous regulations on the manner in which the stock may be issued. Public issuance of securities is beyond the scope of this chapter.

Shareholders

The shareholders have the power to elect directors, amend the bylaws, and approve fundamental changes to the corporation. As noted earlier, a corporation's initial directors are named in the Articles of Incorporation. The shareholders may, however, elect new directors to replace the initial directors. Both the board of directors and the shareholders generally have the power to amend the bylaws. The shareholders must approve all fundamental changes to the corporation, such as merger, a sale of corporate assets outside the ordinary course of business, and dissolution.

Directors

Corporations are required to hold annual meetings. At these annual meetings, the shareholders elect directors. The board of directors will consist of one or more persons, as specified in the corporation's articles or bylaws. The board of directors has general responsibility for the management of the business and affairs of the corporation. The board may hold regular or special meetings for the purpose of conducting its affairs. If a quorum is present (generally a majority of directors), the affirmative vote of a majority of directors present is the act of the board, unless the articles or bylaws require the vote of a greater number. Any action required or permitted to be taken at a directors' meeting may be taken without a meeting if the action is taken by all directors, each of whom must sign a written consent.

The directors are fiduciaries of the corporation. This means that they have to put the corporation's interests ahead of their own. If they fail to do so, they may be personally liable to the shareholders or the corporation for damages.

Officers

The directors usually delegate their day-to-day management duties to the officers. Most corporations have a president, vice-president, secretary and treasurer. The board can appoint such other officers or assistant officers as may be required. The duties of the officers are set forth in the corporation's bylaws, or as specified by the board. The officers are agents of the corporation and act on its behalf. The president generally has the authority to enter into contracts and otherwise act on behalf of the corporation in the ordinary course of corporate affairs.

The board determines the salaries paid to the officers, and the other terms of the officers' employment. It is not unusual for the officers to have employment contracts with the corporation.

Annual Reports

The corporation is required to file an Annual Report & Certificate of Disclosure with the Arizona Corporation Commission. The document is furnished by the corporation commission and may be filed by the corporation electronically. As of this writing, the annual report filing fee is $45. For additional information, the reader may wish to visit the Arizona Corporation Commission's Web site, www.cc.state.az.us, or call the annual reports section, (602) 542-3285.

87

S Corporations

The ABCs of S Corporations

A corporation will, for tax purposes, be either a "C corpora-tion" or an "S corporation." In the majority of cases, it is more beneficial to the corporation and its shareholders to elect to be an S corporation. Before we discuss the benefits of an S corpo-ration, however, we should look at the differences between the two types of corporations.

C Corporations

All corporations in the U.S. start out as C corporations for tax purposes. Some qualified corporations may elect to be S corporations (see discussion below), but the election is not automatic and it does not take effect until it is accepted by the IRS.

A C corporation is taxed as an entity separate from its shareholders. It must pay income taxes on any profit that it makes. The shareholders also have to pay taxes on the corpo-ration's profits when they are distributed. (The profits may not be distributed to the shareholders in the year in which they are earned, for a variety of reasons.) This system results in double taxation, because the corporation's distributions are treated as income to the shareholders, even though the corporation has already paid taxes on its profits.

S Corporations

S corporations are not subject to double taxation, because the corporation's profits and losses flow through to the shareholders. The shareholders pay taxes on the profits in the year in which they are earned. If there are losses, the shareholders may offset the losses against current income. This system taxes the corporation's profits like a partnership, and yet provides the legal advantages of a corporation. (For a discussion about the advantages of the corporate form, please refer to the preceding chapter.)

As mentioned above, there are a number of restrictions on S corporations. To elect to be an S corporation, a corporation must: 1) be a domestic corporation or a domestic entity eligible to be treated as a corporation; 2) not have more than 100 shareholders (husband and wife are treated as one); 3) generally have only individuals as shareholders; 4) not have nonresident alien shareholders; 5) have only one class of stock; 6) not be an ineligible corporation, as defined by the IRS; 7) have a tax year ending December 31, or a different tax year approved by the IRS; and 8) have each shareholder's written consent.

An S election is made by the filing of IRS Form 2553 with the IRS. The election will be accepted by the IRS only if all of the requirements in the preceding paragraph are met. The election should be filed no more than two months and 15 days after the beginning of the tax year for which it is to take effect, or at any time during the tax year preceding the tax year it is to take effect. The tax year of a newly formed corporation starts on the date that it has shareholders, acquires assets, or begins doing business, whichever happens first. If an election is filed late, it will be effective for the next tax year.

Illustration: If a corporation with a tax year beginning January 1 files Form 2553 in April, the S election will be effective for the corporation's next tax year because it was filed too late to be effective for the tax year in which it was filed.

For more information on S corporations, the reader may wish to visit the IRS's Web site, www.irs.gov. Instructions and forms concerning S corporations can be downloaded from the site.

88

Non-Profit Corporations

*Organizations that use surplus revenues
to achieve specific goals*

Non-profit corporations are everywhere. In Arizona, there are about 40,000 non-profit corporations. Typically they are engaged in charitable, religious or scientific activities. They look like the local food bank, church, and Rotary club. In this chapter, we will examine the process of forming and operating an Arizona non-profit corporation.

Difference between Non-profit and Tax Exempt

Non-profit status is a state law concept. Non-profit status may make an organization eligible for certain benefits, such as state sales, property and income tax exemptions. Although most federal tax-exempt organizations are also non-profit organizations, organizing as a non-profit corporation at the state level does not automatically grant the organization exemption from federal income tax. To qualify as exempt from federal income taxes, an organization must meet the requirements set forth in the Internal Revenue Code. For more information on tax exempt organizations and applying for tax-exempt status, please go to www.irs.gov/charities.

Incorporation

One or more persons may incorporate a non-profit corporation. A non-profit corporation may be either tax exempt or non-tax exempt. The incorporators must file articles of incorporation and a certificate of disclosure with the Arizona Corporation Commission. The articles of incorporation must contain: (1) a corporate name; (2) a brief statement of the character of affairs that the corporation initially intends to conduct; (3) the name and address of the initial directors; (4) the name, address and signature of the statutory agent; (5) the street address of the corporation; (6) the name and address of each incorporator; (7) whether or not the corporation will have members; (8) any provision elected by the incorporators; and (9) the signature of each incorporator. The articles of incorporation may contain other provisions, but only the nine items listed are required.

The certificate of disclosure must set forth specific information regarding all of the initial officers, directors, trustees and incorporators. The required information relates generally to prior felony convictions, fraud, and bankruptcy. The certificate of disclosure must be signed by all of the incorporators and contain a declaration by each signer that the signer swears to its contents under penalty of law. A person who intentionally makes any untrue statement of material fact or withholds any material fact with regard to the information required in the certificate, except for information regarding other corporations, is guilty of a felony.

The filing fee for an Arizona non-profit corporation is $40.00 for regular filing, and $95 for expedited filing. The fee must be paid when the articles of incorporation and certificate of disclosure are filed. For additional information on the filing process and for forms, the reader is advised to visit the Corporation Division's Web site, www.azcc.gov/divisions/corporations/filings/forms/index.asp, or call the Phoenix office: (602) 542-3026, or the Tucson office: (520) 628-6560.

Within 60 days after the commission has approved the filing, a copy of the articles of incorporation must be published.

An affidavit evidencing the publication must be filed with the commission within 90 days after the approval date. Once that is done, the incorporation process is complete.

Organization and Operation of the Non-profit Corporation

After incorporation, the board of directors must hold a meeting to complete the organization of the corporation by appointing officers, adopting bylaws, and carrying on any other business brought before the meeting. The bylaws of the corporation may contain any provision for regulating and managing the affairs of the corporation that is not inconsistent with law or the articles of incorporation.

The articles of incorporation or bylaws may establish criteria or procedures for the admission of members and continuation of membership. No person shall be admitted as a member without his consent. A non-profit corporation is not required to have members, however.

Members

A member of a corporation is not personally liable for the acts, debts, liabilities or obligations of the corporation. A member may, however, become liable to the corporation for dues, assessments, and fees (e.g., members of a homeowners association). A member is deemed to have agreed to the liability if, at the time the member becomes a member, there exists a provision of the articles of incorporation, the bylaws, the declaration of a condominium or a planned community or a resolution adopted by the board authorizing or imposing dues, assessments or fees. A home buyer may implicitly consent to liability for dues, assessments and fees. See Chapter 91 on Homeowners Associations.

Unless otherwise provided in the articles of incorporation or bylaws, a corporation with members must hold a membership meeting annually. It may hold regular membership meetings at the times stated in the bylaws. A corporation with members may also hold a special meeting of the members, if the meeting is properly called and noticed. Any action that the corporation may take at any annual, regular, or special meeting of members may be taken without a meeting if the corporation delivers a written ballot to every member entitled to vote on the matter, unless the use of written ballots is prohibited or limited by the articles of incorporation or bylaws.

Directors and Officers

Each corporation must have a board of directors. A board of directors must consist of at least one person. The number of directors will be specified in the articles of incorporation or bylaws. All corporate powers are required to be exercised by or under the authority of its board of directors; and the affairs of the corporation must be managed under the direction of the board. The articles of incorporation or bylaws may prescribe qualifications for directors. A director need not be a resident of Arizona unless the articles or bylaws so require. If the corporation has members, the members will elect the directors. If the corporation does not have members, the directors will be elected or appointed as provided in the articles of incorporation or bylaws. Each director generally serves a term of one year. A director may resign at any time by delivering written notice to the board of directors, its presiding officer or the corporation.

A corporation must have the officers described in its articles of incorporation or bylaws or appointed by the board of directors. The same individual may simultaneously hold more than one office in a corporation (e.g., secretary and treasurer). Each officer must perform the duties set forth by the bylaws, the duties prescribed by the board of directors, or by direction of an officer appointed by the board to prescribe the duties. An officer may resign at any time by delivering notice to the corporation. A board of directors may remove any officer at any time with or without cause.

Standards of Conduct for Directors and Officers

The duties of a director and an officer must be discharged (a) in good faith; (b) with the care that an ordinarily prudent person in a like position would exercise under similar circumstances; and (c) in a manner the director or officer reasonably believes to be in the best interests of the corporation. A director or officer is not liable for any action taken as a director or officer or any failure to take any action if his duties were performed in compliance with the foregoing standards of conduct.

A corporation is authorized to indemnify (to secure against loss) a director or officer in certain cases, and it is required to do so in other cases, all as set forth in the statutes (A.R.S. Sections 10-3850 through 10-3858). In addition, a corporation may purchase insurance on behalf of its officers and directors. This type of insurance is frequently referred to as "errors and omissions" insurance and it typically covers most actions taken as a director or officer or any failure to take action.

Records and Reports

A corporation is required to keep as permanent records minutes of all meetings of its members and board of directors, a record of all actions taken by the members or directors without a meeting, and a record of all actions taken by committees. A corporation must also maintain appropriate accounting records, and a record of its members. These and other records must be kept at the corporation's principal office, its known place of business, or at the office of its statutory agent. Subject to certain limitations, any person who has been a member of record for at least six months may inspect and copy any of the corporation's records.

Every corporation is required to file an annual report and certificate of disclosure with the Arizona Corporation Commission, and to pay an annual fee. The annual fee is $10. Annual report instructions and forms are available online at the commission's Web site, www.cc.state.az.us/divisions/corporations/annrpts/arinstruct.asp. Failure to file the annual report constitutes grounds for administrative dissolution of the corporation.

89

Limited Liability Companies

*A member's liability is limited to his investment
in the company.*

The concept of a limited liability company is relatively new. In 1992, Arizona adopted the Arizona Limited Liability Company Act. The Act authorizes the use of a business form called the limited liability company, commonly abbreviated "L.L.C." Prior to the adoption of the Act, limited liability companies did not exist in Arizona or most other states. Now, all 50 states have adopted acts authorizing the formation and operation of limited liability companies. In Arizona, according to statistics published by the Corporation Commission, there are about half a million L.L.C.'s, as compared to about 160,000 business corporations.

There are three basic forms of business organizations in Arizona: corporations, partnerships, and limited liability companies. A limited liability company is a hybrid business form that offers favorable characteristics of both a corporation and a partnership (corporations and partnerships are discussed in Chapters 86 and 90, respectively). An L.L.C. gives its owners the "best of both worlds," so to speak, by providing them with the limited liability of a corporation and the favorable income tax treatment of a partnership. If properly organized, an L.L.C. is not subject to federal or state income taxation; instead, the owners of the company are taxed on its profits.

A limited liability company may be organized in Arizona

to conduct any lawful activity, except banking or insurance, and can even be organized to engage in professional services, such as accounting, engineering, law or medicine. An L.L.C. is formed by filing "articles of organization" with the Arizona Corporation Commission, and paying a filing fee in the amount of $50 for regular filing, and $85 for expedited filing. (These fees are always subject to change.)

An L.L.C. must be formed with one or more "members," which are similar to the shareholders of a corporation or the partners of a partnership. A member's liability for the company's debts and obligations is generally limited to the amount of his investment, which is similar to the limited liability afforded to a corporate shareholder.

The affairs of an L.L.C. and the conduct of its business normally will be governed by an operating agreement among the members. Although the Act does not require that an L.L.C. have an operating agreement, a written operating agreement is advisable because it controls the management of the company, profit and loss-sharing arrangements, and all other commercially important matters. A carefully drafted operating agreement may also determine whether the company receives favorable classification as a partnership for federal income tax purposes.

Limited liability companies have a couple of distinct advantages over traditional business forms. First, an L.L.C. is not required to file annual reports or pay annual fees to the state. A corporation is required to do both. Second, an L.L.C. may be structured so that the members participate in the management of the business without losing their limited liability. A limited partner involved in a traditional limited partnership, by contrast, may lose his liability protection if he takes part in the management of the limited partnership's business.

A limited liability company is often the ideal business form for a family-owned business or an enterprise with a small number of investors. The ever-increasingly popular L.L.C. has replaced the corporation as the dominant form of business for non-publicly traded entities in Arizona.

90

Partnerships

Partnership: a marriage made for business

A partnership is an association of two or more persons to carry on, as co-owners, a business for profit, whether or not the persons intended to form a partnership.

A partnership is an entity distinct from its partners. It may conduct business in Arizona under a fictitious name, subject to the requirement that it file a fictitious name certificate. (For additional information concerning fictitious names, please refer to Chapter 93.) A partnership may sue and be sued in the name of the partnership. In these respects, a partnership is similar to a corporation or a limited liability company.

Under Arizona law, there are different types of partnerships. This chapter deals with general partnerships. Limited partnerships, limited liability partnerships, limited foreign liability partnerships, and professional limited liability partnerships, while all partnerships, too, are outside the scope of this chapter.

Unlike other forms of business entities (*e.g.,* corporations and limited liability companies), there is no requirement that a partnership file any organizational documents with the state of Arizona. A partnership may literally be formed with a handshake. A better practice, however, is to have a written partnership agreement. A partnership agreement is an agreement among the partners concerning the partnership. It may be written, oral, or implied.

The place from which the main part of the partnership's business is managed is called the "chief executive office." It may be the home of one of the partners, or a more traditional business office. A partnership is required to keep its books and records at its chief executive office. It is also required to provide partners and their agents access to its books and records.

Each partner has equal rights in the management and conduct of the partnership business. A difference arising as to a matter in the ordinary course of business will be decided by a majority of the partners. An act *outside* the ordinary course of business may be undertaken only with the consent of *all* of the partners.

The partners owe one another the duty of loyalty, the duty of care, and the obligation of good faith and fair dealing. Each partner and the partnership must generally furnish to a partner all important information concerning the partnership's business and affairs. A partner's failure to disclose this information constitutes a breach of his fiduciary duty. (For a discussion on partners' fiduciary duties and actions for breach, please refer to Chapter 78.)

Each partner is entitled to an equal share of the partnership profits and is chargeable with a share of the partnership losses in proportion to his share of the profits. For tax purposes, partners are considered to be self-employed. A partner's distributive share of the partnership's income or loss from carrying on a trade or business is net earnings from self-employment. A partnership with profits or losses must file a federal income tax return. (For more information on the tax aspects of a partnership, the reader may wish to obtain IRS Publication 541, *Partnerships*. This publication and partnership tax forms may be downloaded from the IRS's Web site, www.irs.gov.)

Each partner is an agent of the partnership for purposes of its business. A partnership may file, with the Arizona Secretary of State, a statement of partnership authority. This statement may state the authority, or limitations on the authority, of some or all of the partners to enter into transactions on behalf of the partnership and any other matter.

A partnership is liable for loss or injury caused to a person by the conduct of a partner acting in the ordinary course of partnership business, or with authority of the partnership. Generally, all partners are liable for all obligations of the partnership. This is referred to as personal liability.

Legal Tip:

Personal liability can be avoided or limited by the use of another form of business entity (*e.g.*, corporation, limited liability company, limited partnership, or limited liability partnership). For this reason, partnerships should be *avoided* whenever possible. However, because a partnership may be formed regardless of whether the persons intended to form one, anyone who receives a share of the profits of a business should take steps to ensure that a partnership was not inadvertently formed (and, if one was, convert it to another form of business entity).

91

Homeowners Associations

"A man's home is his castle"

A homeowners association is a nonprofit corporation or unincorporated association created pursuant to a declaration (commonly called a "declaration of covenants, conditions and restrictions"). In those communities that have homeowners associations--and there are thousands of them across the state--membership in the association is mandatory and community documents impose restrictions on the use of the properties within the community.

Associations exist for both condominiums and planned communities. Although the associations for condominiums and planned communities are both commonly referred to as "homeowners associations," the associations are subject to slightly different laws. Because considerably more people live in planned communities than condominiums in the state, this chapter is based on the laws applicable to planned communities.

Assessments and Violations

A homeowners association has the power under the declaration to assess association members the costs and expenses incurred in the performance of the association's obligations under the declaration (typically, the upkeep of common areas and enforcement of deed restrictions).

An association may not impose a regular assessment that is more than twenty percent greater than the immediately preceding fiscal year's assessment without the approval of the majority of its members. In most cases, the association's board of directors may impose reasonable charges for the late payment of assessments. A payment by a member is deemed late if it is unpaid fifteen or more days after its due date, unless the community documents provide for a longer period. Charges for the late payment are limited to the greater of $15 or ten percent of the amount of the unpaid assessment.

The association's board of directors may impose reasonable monetary penalties on members for violations of the declaration, bylaws and rules of the association, after giving the member the opportunity to be heard. The board of directors may not impose a late charge for an unpaid penalty that exceeds the greater of $15 or ten percent of the unpaid penalty. A payment is deemed late if it is unpaid fifteen or more days after its due date, unless the community documents provide for a longer period.

A member who receives a written notice that the condition of his property is in violation of the community documents may provide the association with a written response (by certified mail) within ten business days after the date of the notice. The association, within ten business days after receipt of the response, must respond to the member with a written explanation regarding the notice. The notice must contain specific information regarding the violation, as set forth in the statutes. Unless the required information is provided, the association cannot proceed with any action to enforce the community documents. At any time before or after the exchange of information, the member may petition for an administrative hearing (discussed below) if the dispute is within the jurisdiction of the department of fire, building and life safety.

Open Meetings and Records

All meetings of the association, board of directors, and any regularly scheduled committee meetings are open to all members of the association or any member's designated representative. All members and designated representatives so desiring must be permitted to speak at an appropriate time during the deliberations and proceedings. Persons attending may tape record or videotape those portions of the meetings of the board of directors and meetings of the members that are open. Any portion of a meeting may be closed only if that portion is limited to consideration of certain legal matters, personal member information, or association employee matters. The association must hold a meeting at least once a year. Special meetings of the association may be called upon proper notice to the members.

All meetings of a planned community generally must be conducted openly and notices and agenda must be provided for those meetings that contain the information that is reasonably necessary to inform the members of the matters to be discussed or decided and to ensure that members have the ability to speak after discussion of agenda items, but before a vote of the board of directors is taken.

With limited exception, all financial and other records of the association must be made reasonably available for examination by any member or his designated representative. The association may not charge a member for making material available for review. The association has ten business days to fulfill a request for examination.

The board of directors must provide for an annual financial audit, review or compilation of the association. The audit, review or compilation must be completed no later than 180 days after the end of the association's fiscal year and must be made available upon request to the members within thirty days after its completion.

In communities with fewer than 50 units, a member must mail or deliver to a purchaser within ten days after receipt of a written notice of pending sale of the unit copies of the community documents and a dated statement containing certain information regarding the association. The information required to be furnished is described in A.R.S. Section 33-1806. In communities with 50 or more units, the association is obligated to furnish the required information, but it may charge the member statutorily prescribed fees to do so.

Lien for Assessments

The association has a lien on a unit for any assessment levied against that unit from the time the assessment becomes due. The association's lien for assessments, for charges for late payment of those assessments, for reasonable collection fees and for reasonable attorney fees and costs incurred with respect to those assessments may be foreclosed, but only if the owner has been delinquent in the payment of assessments for one year or in the amount of $1,200, whichever occurs first. The association's lien for monies other than for assessments, for charges for late payment of those assessments, for reasonable collection fees and for reasonable attorney fees and costs incurred with respect to those assessments may not be foreclosed and is effective only on conveyance of an interest in the property.

Homeowners' Rights

Under Arizona law, an association may not prohibit certain activities within the community that it governs. Some of those activities include:

- Display of the American flag or military flag, if the flag is displayed in a manner consistent with the federal flag code.
- Display of the POW/MIA flag.
- Display of the Arizona state flag, or an Arizona Indian nations flag.
- Display of the Gadsden flag.
- The indoor or outdoor display of a political sign on the member's property, within 45 days before an election and seven days after an election.
- The use of cautionary signs regarding children.
- Children engaging in recreational activity on residential roadways that are under the association's

jurisdiction and on which the posted speed is twenty-five miles per hour or less.

- The indoor or outdoor display of a for sale sign on the member's property.
- The circulation of political petitions.
- The installation or use of a solar energy device.

Although the association may not prohibit the above activities, in most cases it may enact rules regulating a particular activity that are not inconsistent with the statutes.

Administrative Hearings to Resolve Disputes

The Legislature recently passed legislation providing for the administrative resolution of disputes between homeowners and associations. The new law does not limit the rights of the parties to pursue matters in the legal system, but it provides an alternative. The owner or association may petition the department of fire, building and life safety for a hearing concerning violations of community documents or the statutes that regulate planned communities. The petition must be in writing on a form approved by the department and accompanied by a nonrefundable filing fee. The filing fee for a single violation (disputed issue) is $550; for multiple violations it is $2,000. The amount of the filing fee is subject to change. For current fees and forms, the reader is invited to visit the department's Web site, www.dfbls.az.gov/hoa.aspx.

The department does not have authority to hear any dispute among or between owners to which the association is not a party.

On receipt of the petition and the filing fee, the department must mail (by certified mail) a copy of the petition along with notice to the other party that a response is required within twenty days. After receiving the response, the petition will be referred to the office of administrative hearings for a hearing. Failure to file a response will result in the issuance of a default decision in favor of the petitioner.

An administrative law judge will hear all contested matters.

After a hearing, the judge will issue an order. If the party who filed the petition prevails at the hearing, the administrative law judge will order the other party to reimburse the winning party the filing fee paid. The order issued by the administrative law judge may be appealed to the Arizona Superior Court.

92

Registration of Trade Names and Trademarks

*"Imitation is the sincerest form of flattery." —*Proverb

A trade name is the name under which a person or company conducts business. A trademark is a word, name, symbol or device, or any combination of these items, that is used by a person or company to identify its goods, and to distinguish them from goods made or sold by others.[1] (If a mark is used to identify services, as opposed to goods, it is called a "service mark." The same principles apply to both trademarks and service marks.)

Trade names and trademarks may be registered, for a small fee, with the Arizona Secretary of State. If a company does business in more than one state or is engaged in interstate commerce, it may also register its trade name and/or trademark with the U.S. Patent and Trademark Office. This chapter is primarily intended to assist persons and companies who may wish to register their trade names and/or trademarks under Arizona's registration laws.

Trade Names

The form to apply for registration of a trade name is furnished by the Arizona Secretary of State. It requires the disclosure of certain information concerning the person applying for registration (the "applicant"), the name, title or designation to be registered, the nature of the applicant's business, and the length of time the name has been used.

The Secretary of State will not file an application for registration of a trade name if it might mislead the public, or is not readily distinguishable from another registered trade name still in effect. The Secretary of State also will not file an application for registration of a trade name that is the same as, or "deceptively similar to," an existing corporate name.

The Secretary of State maintains a list of all registered trade names in Arizona. A registered name search can be conducted online, by logging on to the Secretary of State's Web site, www. azsos.gov, and clicking on Business Filings/Trade Names and Trademarks/Search for Registered Names.

If the Secretary of State accepts an application for registration of a trade name, he will issue a certificate of registration to the applicant. The trade name registration is effective for a period of five years. The registration may, however, be renewed for successive five-year periods.

The registration of a trade name will generally give to the owner of the name exclusive right to the use of the name. However, registration of a trade name does not affect the rights of a person or company that is already using the trade name in the operation of its business.

Any trade name may be assigned by the owner to another person. To assign a trade name, the owner must execute a written assignment and file it with the Secretary of State. The Secretary of State will then issue a new certificate of registration to the new owner for the remainder of the term of the registration.

Trademarks

Any person or company who adopts and uses a trademark in Arizona may file, with the Arizona Secretary of State, an application for registration of the trademark. The Secretary of State will provide the application form. The application must contain certain information about the applicant, the goods in connection with which the mark is used, and when the mark was first used. It must also include a statement that the applicant is the owner of the mark and that no other person has the right to use the mark in Arizona in the identical form, or in such near resemblance to the mark as might be calculated to deceive or to be mistaken for it. The application must be accompanied by a specimen or facsimile of the trademark in triplicate.

If the application is accepted for filing, the Secretary of State will issue to the applicant a certificate of registration. The certificate is legal proof of the registration of the trademark in any Arizona court.

Registration of the trademark is effective for a term of 10 years. The registration may be renewed for successive periods of 10 years, by the timely filing of renewal applications with the Secretary of State.

Any mark and its registration will be assignable with the goodwill of the business in which the mark is used or with that part of the goodwill of the business connected with the mark. To assign a trademark, the owner must execute a written assignment. The assignment should be filed within three months after its execution with the Arizona Secretary of State, who, in turn, will issue a new registration certificate for the remainder of the term.

The owner of a trademark that is famous in Arizona may obtain a court order prohibiting another person's commercial use of the mark. To obtain a court order, the owner must show that the other person's use of the trademark began after the mark became famous and causes dilution of the distinctive quality of the mark. In determining whether a trademark is distinctive and famous, a court may consider, among other things, whether the trademark is registered. If a person willfully intends to trade on the owner's reputation or to cause dilution of a famous mark, then, in addition to prohibiting use of the mark, the owner may sue that person for money damages.

Legal Tips:

Trade names and trademarks are considered intellectual property, and should be protected to the greatest extent possible. Both proper use and registration of trade names and trademarks are important steps in this process.

Another critical consideration is to select a name/mark that can be protected against a third party's use. Do not choose a merely descriptive name (*e.g.,* apple for fruit), but rather choose a more fanciful term (*e.g.,* apple for computers). This will help to insure that your mark is considered distinctive for the relevant goods or services in the marketplace.

If a trademark is used beyond the borders of Arizona (in interstate commerce, for instance), federal registration should be considered. State registration provides only limited territorial protection. A federal trademark registration provides the trademark owner with the right to expand its use of the trademark nationwide.

A trademark search is a prudent step to take before a new trademark is adopted to determine if you have the right to use the trademark. A nationwide clearance search should be conducted prior to the adoption of any mark to prevent disruption of your business that would result from being required to change your trademark by a prior user of a similar trademark. A court may order you to stop using a trademark if you adopt the trademark after another has used or registered the same trademark for a similar product or service. The test for trademark infringement is whether the use of the trademark would create a likelihood of confusion in the marketplace.

For additional information or forms, the reader may wish to visit the Arizona Secretary of State's Web site, www.azsos. gov. Trademarks that are federally registered may be searched on the U.S. Patent and Trademark Office Web site, www.uspto. gov.

93

Fictitious Name Certificates

"No, Groucho is not my real name. I'm breaking it in for a friend." —Comedian Groucho Marx

Many individuals and companies do business under fictitious names. A fictitious name simply is a name different from the true name of the business owner. The law requires that those doing business under a fictitious name in Arizona record a fictitious name certificate.

The statutes in question are intended to provide disclosure of the true identity of the business owner and prevent fraud. They require any person, corporation or partnership transacting business in Arizona under a fictitious name or a designation not showing the name of the owner to record a fictitious name certificate with the county recorder of the county in which the place of business is located. If the business is a sole proprietorship, the certificate must state the name of the owner of the business and his place of residence, and it must be signed by the owner and acknowledged. If the business is a corporation, the certificate must state the name and address of the corporation, and it must be signed by the corporation's statutory agent and acknowledged. If the business is a partnership, the certificate must state the names of all members of the partnership and their place of residence, and it must be signed by the partners and acknowledged.

A new certificate must be recorded upon any change in

ownership of the business, unless the business is a corporation. If a corporation transfers the right to use its fictitious name to another corporation, a new certificate must be recorded.

A person or corporation doing business contrary to these laws cannot bring a lawsuit on a contract or transaction made in the fictitious name until a fictitious name certificate has been recorded.

The above requirements do not apply to a person or corporation that has either filed a trade name certificate with the Secretary of State (discussed in Chapter 92), or obtained authorization from the Arizona Corporation Commission to conduct business as a foreign corporation using a particular name.

94

Restrictive Covenants in Employment

The law does not favor restrictive covenants.

A restriction is a limitation. A covenant is a promise. A restrictive covenant is a promise to limit activities, usually found in an employment agreement. Often, an employer will attempt to impose limitations on his employees' post-employment activities by the use of restrictive covenants.

The law does not favor restrictive covenants in employment relationships. A restrictive covenant generally will be strictly construed against the employer. One reason restrictive covenants are construed against the employer is because the employee is typically at a bargaining disadvantage. Unequal bargaining power may be a factor to consider when examining the hardship on the departing employee.

There are two often-used types of restrictive covenants in employment agreements: 1) covenants not to compete, and 2) non-solicitation covenants. Below, we will look at the law concerning each type of covenant.

1. Covenant Not to Compete

A covenant not to compete restricts an employee's ability to work after his current employment is terminated. Typically, it will prohibit the employee from working in the same trade or industry for a period of time after the termination of his employment, within a specified geographic area. For example, a covenant may state, "John shall not sell widgets for a period of five years after the termination of his employment by Arizona Widget Company within the state of Arizona." Both the term and the geographic scope of the covenant must be reasonable. However, many restrictive covenants are too broad to be valid (such as the covenant in the preceding example, for instance).

Under Arizona law, a covenant not to compete in an employment agreement is "valid and enforceable by injunction when the restraint does not exceed that reasonably necessary to protect the employer's business, is not unreasonably restrictive of the rights of the employee, does not contravene public policy, and is reasonable as to time and space." A restrictive covenant is reasonable and enforceable when it protects some legitimate interest of the employer beyond the mere interest in protecting itself from competition. The legitimate purpose of post-employment restraints is to prevent competitive use of information or relationships which pertain peculiarly to the employer and which the employee acquired in the course of employment.

What is reasonable will turn on a very fact-intensive inquiry and will depend on duration, geographic area and the activity prohibited. Each case hinges on its own particular facts. A restriction is unreasonable and will not be enforced if (a) the restraint is greater than necessary to protect the employer's legitimate interest, or (b) that interest is outweighed by the hardship to the employee and the likely injury to the public. No exact formula can be used when balancing these competing interests.

The burden is on the employer to demonstrate that the restraint is no greater than necessary to protect the employer's legitimate interest, and that such interest is not outweighed by the hardship to the employee. The court in one case found that a three-year covenant was unreasonable and that any provision over six months was unnecessary to protect the employer's interests.

In another case, a restrictive covenant was held to be unenforceable by the court because its statewide scope was overly broad and unreasonably restricted the right of the employee to work in his chosen occupation. Again, the restriction cannot be greater than necessary to protect the employer's legitimate interests. Each case is decided on its own facts.

2. Non-Solicitation Covenant

The second type of restrictive covenant is the non-solicitation, or "anti-piracy" covenant. Unlike the covenant not to compete, it does not restrict the employee's subsequent employment. The non-solicitation covenant restricts the employee's ability to solicit his employer's customers after the termination of his employment. A typical non-solicitation covenant might read: "For a period of two years after Employee's termination with Arizona Widget Company, the Employee agrees that he/she will not solicit or contact for the purpose of establishing a business relationship any of Arizona Widget Company's customers as they exist on the date of Employee's termination." For the reasons discussed below, the two-year period in the preceding example probably is too long to be enforceable.

The non-solicitation provision in Arizona Widget Company's fictional employment agreement is an "anti-piracy" covenant. This type of covenant is designed to prevent former employees from using information learned during their employment to divert or "steal" customers from the former employer. An anti-piracy agreement is ordinarily not deemed unreasonable or oppressive, unless it is so restrictive in its scope that it becomes unenforceable. An anti-piracy agreement is only enforceable as long as it is no broader than necessary to protect the employer's legitimate business interest.

What is reasonable depends on the whole subject matter of the agreement, including the purpose to be accomplished by the restriction and the totality of the circumstances which show the intention of the parties. In the leading Arizona case on the subject, the anti-piracy covenant was held to be unreasonable because it subjected the former employee to a penalty for customers who transferred to the employee's new employer, even if the employee did not solicit the customer.

The burden is on the employer to prove the extent of its protectable interest. The employer's interest in its customer base, however, is balanced with the employee's right to the customers. Where the employee took an active role and brought customers with him to the job, courts are more reluctant to enforce restrictive covenants.

In addition to proving that the anti-piracy covenant is reasonable, the employer must prove that the former employee actually "solicited" customers. Merely informing customers of a change of employer, without more, does not constitute solicitation. Neither does the willingness to discuss business upon invitation of another party. The law will not prohibit a former employee from receiving business initiated by the customers of his former employer, even if the former employee would be prohibited from soliciting such business.

Legal Tip:

If a restrictive covenant is unfair under the circumstances of the case, or if it imposes an extreme hardship on the departed employee, then the restrictive covenant probably is invalid.

95

Employer's Liability for Employee's Actions

Liability without fault

An employer can be legally responsible for the actions of its employees. This is known as *respondeat superior* liability. This liability is imposed without fault on the part of the employer.

To establish this claim, the injured person must prove that: 1) the act was the kind that the employee was employed to perform, 2) the act occurred substantially *within the authorized time and space limits of the employment*, and 3) the act was motivated at least in part by a purpose to serve the employer. An employer may also be liable for the acts of its agents acting outside the scope of their employment under certain circumstances (such as where the employer intended the conduct, or was negligent or reckless).

The central question in most cases is whether or not the employee's conduct was within the scope of employment (see italicized language in the preceding paragraph). The test in Arizona for acting within the scope of employment is fairly broad: "An employee is acting within the scope of his employment while he is doing any reasonable thing which his employment expressly or impliedly authorizes him to do or which may reasonably be said to have been contemplated by that employment as necessarily or probably incidental to the employment."

An employer is generally not responsible for travel by an employee while going to and from the work place (even if the employer pays the employee for travel time). An employee traveling during his lunch hour is usually not acting within the scope of his employment, either.

However, if the employee is also performing a service for the employer that would have necessitated another trip by an employee, the employer will be responsible for that employee's actions. (An employer may be responsible for the acts of an employee who drops off the mail at the post office on his way home from work, for example.) An employer may also be held liable when an employee is involved in an accident while running a special errand for his employer, not involving his normal duties.

Whether an employer is liable for the actions of an employee is generally a question of fact, to be determined on a case-by-case basis. The smart employer will realize when the conduct of its employees may give rise to liability under the doctrine of *respondeat superior*, and have a policy of insurance in place to cover that liability.

96

Payment of Wages

"An honest day's work for an honest day's wages."—Proverb

The payment of wages in Arizona is governed by state law. (Some employers in Arizona will also be governed by the federal Fair Labor Standards Act, but a discussion of the FLSA is beyond the scope of this chapter.) The statutes governing payment of wages and wage claims come into play any time there is a wage dispute between an employer and employee.

It probably makes sense to start this chapter with a definition of "wages." Wages means "nondiscretionary income due an employee in return for labor or services, ... for which the employee had a reasonable expectation of being paid." It is immaterial whether the amount is determined by a time, task, piece, commission or other method of calculation. Wages include sick pay, vacation pay, severance pay, commissions, bonuses and other amounts promised when the employer has a policy or practice of making those payments. Thus, the definition of wages is very broad.

In November 2006, Arizona voters approved an increase in Arizona's minimum wage. At that time, the minimum wage went from $5.15 per hour to $6.75 per hour. That initiative also called for a cost of living increase on January 1 of successive years. As of January 1, 2012, Arizona's minimum wage was $7.65 per hour.

Every employer in Arizona must designate two or more

days in each month, not more than 16 days apart, as fixed paydays for the payment of wages to its employees. Wages must be paid in cash (U.S. currency only), in negotiable bank checks, or, with the written consent of the employee, by deposit to the employee's bank account. When an employee's wages are paid by deposit in a financial institution, he must be furnished with a statement of his earnings and withholdings.

An employer is permitted to personally deliver the wages to the employee no later than five days after the end of the most recent pay period, or deposit the wages in the mail no later than five days after the end of the most recent pay period for delivery to an address specified by the employee. These rules effectively allow an employer to withhold up to five days' wages. Overtime pay must be paid no later than 16 days after the end of the most recent pay period.

The above rules do not apply to employers whose principal place of business is located outside Arizona and whose payroll system is centralized outside the state, to school districts, or to other state agencies. They also do not apply to employees whose salaries are subject to provisions of collective bargaining agreements. The wage statutes are different for these groups.

An employer may withhold wages under the following circumstances:

- The employer is required or empowered to do so by law.
- The employer has the employee's prior written authorization.
- There is a reasonable good faith dispute as to the amount of wages due.

In the case of discharge, special payment rules apply. When an employee is discharged, he must be paid wages due him within three working days or the end of the next regular pay period, *whichever is sooner*. When an employee quits, he must be paid in the usual manner all wages due him no later than the regular payday. If requested by the employee, his wages must be mailed to him.

In that wages include sick pay, vacation pay, severance pay, commissions and bonuses, an employee's last paycheck often will include these extra items. If it does not, the employee may have a valid wage claim.

The wage statutes contain significant penalties for non-compliance. Any employer who fails to pay wages due is guilty of a petty offense, and may be required to pay three times the amount of the unpaid wages, plus costs and attorney's fees.

An employee who is owed wages may file a lawsuit against the employer for three times the amount of unpaid wages, plus his attorney's fees and costs. If the employee wins the lawsuit, he will be awarded a judgment against the employer, on which he can then execute to get paid.

Instead of filing a lawsuit, an employee with a wage claim that does not exceed $2,500 may file a claim with the labor department of the Industrial Commission of Arizona ("Labor Department"). The claim must be filed within one year from when the wages were due.

If the employee chooses to file a wage claim with the Labor Department, he can only claim the amount of wages actually owed. The Labor Department will investigate the wage claim to determine if wages are due or if a dispute exists between the parties. The employer will be notified of the wage claim and may file a response to it.

Upon completion of its investigation, the Labor Department will notify the parties of its findings. If it is determined that the claim is valid, the Labor Department will direct that the unpaid wages be paid. The Labor Department's determination can only be appealed to the superior court. If neither party seeks review of the Labor Department's determination, it will become final.

If the Labor Department finds that there is a dispute that cannot be resolved by investigation, the employee may attempt to recover the amount of wages claimed by filing a lawsuit against the employer. An employer who has been ordered by the Labor Department or a court to pay wages and who fails to do so within 10 days after the order becomes final must pay, as a penalty, three times the amount of the unpaid wages, plus interest at the legal rate.

For additional information or forms, the reader may wish to visit the Labor Department's Web site, www.ica.state.az.us/Labor/labor_main.aspx, or call (602) 542-4515 (Phoenix); (520) 628-5459 (Tucson).

97

Unemployment Insurance

"The Unemployment Insurance Program provides a measure of economic security to the individual worker and to the community when unemployment beyond the worker's control occurs." — Public Policy Statement

Arizona has an unemployment insurance (UI) program for the benefit of unemployed workers. The cost of benefits paid to unemployed workers is funded by UI taxes paid by Arizona employers. The UI Program is administered by the Arizona Department of Economic Security.

Employers' Duties

Every employer in Arizona, with limited exceptions, must pay state and federal unemployment taxes.[2] An employer who pays Arizona Unemployment Taxes is allowed to take a credit against its Federal Unemployment Tax. This credit reduces the Federal Unemployment Taxes payable by an employer to 0.6% from 6.0%. An employer must pay state unemployment taxes on the first $7,000 in wages paid to each employee in a calendar year ("taxable wages").

Employers in Arizona are required to report both gross and taxable wages on Form UC-018, Unemployment Tax & Wage Report. These reports are due on the last day of the month following the end of the previous quarter. (Most Arizona employers receive preprinted quarterly reports by mail in advance of the filing deadline.) If a quarterly wage report is not timely filed, the employer will be assessed a late report penalty of up to $200, and interest of 1% per month on the late payment.

For more information, an employer should obtain the Arizona Employer's Handbook from the Arizona Department of Economic Security. The Handbook may be obtained from DES online, at www.azdes.gov.

Employees' Benefits

An employee who becomes unemployed may file a claim for UI benefits. To be eligible for benefits, the employee must have wages in at least two quarters of his base period. The base period is the first four of the last five completed calendar quarters from the date the claim is filed. (For example, if a claim is filed in March, the base period will be the 12-month period, prior to filing the claim, from October 1 through September 30.)

An employee must meet certain other requirements to be eligible for UI benefits. The employee must be able to work, available for work, willing to accept suitable work, actively seeking employment, and be out of work through no fault of his own. If an employee voluntarily quits his job, he must show that he quit for good cause. If an employee is terminated or discharged, his employer must show that he was terminated for work-related misconduct. (Thus, an employee who is terminated for theft or dishonesty will not be eligible for UI benefits, regardless of his ability or desire to work.)

After an employee files an initial claim for benefits, he will receive a Wage Statement which lists all of the wages paid by his base period employers, and also shows the weekly and total amount of benefits that he may receive if he meets all of the eligibility requirements. Weekly benefits range from $60 to $240, calculated from the employee's highest quarter base period earnings. An employee may draw UI benefits for up to 26 weeks in the year following his unemployment, depending on how much he earned in his base period.

98

Workers' Compensation

*An employer who fails to obtain coverage
may be ordered to stop doing business.*

The workers' compensation laws provide for the payment of compensation to workers who are injured on the job in Arizona. These laws provide an insurance fund and a schedule of benefits for workers engaged in manual or mechanical labor who are injured in the course of their employment. Employers subject to the workers' compensation laws are required to provide workers' compensation insurance to their employees.

Liability for Injuries

Except as discussed below, an employer who provides workers' compensation insurance is not liable for damages for injury or death of an employee, unless the employee rejected the workers' compensation coverage. If an employee rejects the employer's workers' compensation coverage, that employee retains the right to sue the employer for workplace injuries. To reject the coverage and retain the right to sue, an employee must give written notice to the employer *before* the injuries are sustained by him. An employer who receives such a notice from an employee must file it with his insurance carrier within five days.

An employer who fails to provide workers' compensation insurance may be sued for work injuries. In any action brought by an injured employee, proof of the injury will be evidence of negligence on the part of the employer and *the burden will be on the employer to show freedom from negligence resulting in the injury.*

Every employer, except those in exempt occupations, must post and keep posted in a conspicuous place upon his premises, in English and Spanish and available for inspection by all workers, a notice advising employees of their right to reject the provisions of the compulsory compensation law. An employer must also advise employees that blank forms of notice are available to all employees at the office of the company. The required notice forms are available from any Arizona workers' compensation insurance carrier.

If an employer fails to post and keep posted the notice required by law, or fails to keep available at the place where the employees are hired the blank forms of notice to be signed by the employee, it will be optional for an injured employee to accept compensation under the workers' compensation law or to sue the employer in court for personal injury damages.

Payments from the Special Fund

An injured worker may file a claim for workers' compensation benefits with the Industrial Commission of Arizona (ICA). If the employer is not insured, the employee will be paid benefits identical to those paid by insurance carriers from the ICA's Special Fund. The employer will be notified by the ICA of his liability to the Special Fund, and this notice will include a penalty of 10% of the amount paid from the Special Fund or $1,000, whichever is greater, plus interest on the amount expended. The payments made from the Special Fund and penalty act as a judgment against the employer.

Sanctions for Failure to Secure Coverage

An employer who fails to obtain coverage for his employees may be ordered by the court to stop doing business until he complies with the law and provides workers' compensation coverage. In addition, the ICA may assess a civil penalty on an employer who is not insured as required by law.

Employer's Duties after Injury or Death

Every employer who is required to furnish workers' compensation insurance must file with the ICA and his insurance carrier a written report of every injury or death. In the case of death, the report must be filed within 24 hours. In the case of injury or disease, the report must be filed within 10 days after receiving notice of the accident. The report form may be obtained from the workers' compensation carrier or the ICA. (It can also be downloaded from the ICA's Web site, www.ica. state.az.us.)

Upon learning of an accident resulting in injury to an employee, the employer must provide the employee with the name and address of the employer's insurance carrier, the policy number, and the expiration date.

Inspection of Records

The employer's books, records and payrolls must always remain open to the ICA or its assistants, in order for it to administer the law. An employer who refuses to submit his books, records and payroll for inspection may be penalized in the amount of $500 for each offense. A commissioner may enter any place of employment to collect facts and statistics, and his admittance may not be refused by an employer.

Unfair Claim Processing and Bad Faith

The ICA has authority to investigate complaints of unfair claim processing practices or bad faith by an employer. If the ICA finds that unfair claim processing or bad faith occurred in the handling of a claim, it will award the claimant, in addition to any benefits it finds are due and owing, a benefit penalty of 25% of the benefit amount ordered to be paid or $500, whichever is more. If the ICA finds that an employer has a history or pattern of repeated unfair claim processing practices or bad faith, it may impose a penalty of up to $1,000 for each violation.

99

Interest Rates

"It is not my interest to pay the principal, nor my principle to pay the interest." —Richard Brinsley Sheridan

Rates of interest may be established by private contract or by law.

In Arizona, interest on any loan, indebtedness, or other obligation will be at the rate of 10% per annum, unless a different rate is contracted for in writing, in which event any rate of interest may be agreed to. Interest on any judgment that is based on a written agreement evidencing a loan, indebtedness or obligation that bears a rate of interest not in excess of the maximum permitted by law will be at the rate of interest provided in the agreement and must be specified in the judgment.

Unless specifically provided for in a statute or a different rate is contracted for in writing, interest on a judgment will be at the lesser of 10% per annum or at a rate per annum that is equal to one percent above the prime rate in effect on the date that the judgment is entered. The judgment must state the applicable interest rate, and it will not change after it is entered.

Certain types of lenders and interest on certain types of loans are governed by statute. Examples of these include premium finance companies and consumer lenders, both of which are prohibited from making certain types of loans having a rate of interest greater than thirty-six percent per annum.

Under the "Rule of 72," an obligation bearing interest at the statutory rate of 10% per annum will double in amount in 7.2 years. (To determine how long it will take to double the principal amount, simply divide the interest rate into 72. The resulting number will be the number of years required.)

Note: A person who makes an interest-free loan or a reduced interest loan may be deemed by the IRS to have made a gift. The IRS will "impute" a rate of interest in such cases.

100

Contracts That Must Be in Writing

Arizona's Statute of Frauds

The Arizona State Legislature, to prevent fraud, enacted a law requiring that certain promises or agreements be in writing. The statute is aptly named the Statute of Frauds. No action may be brought in court to enforce a promise or agreement that is covered by the Statute of Frauds, unless the person to be charged (or someone lawfully authorized by him) has signed a writing containing the promise or agreement.

In the absence of a signed writing, no court action may be brought:

- To charge an executor or administrator for certain estate-related debts.
- To charge a person upon a promise to pay the debt of another.
- To charge a person upon an agreement made upon consideration of marriage, except a mutual promise to marry.
- Upon a contract to sell goods having a value of $500 or more, unless the buyer accepts the goods or gives something to bind the contract, or unless certain auction sale rules apply.
- Upon an agreement which is not performed within one year.

- Upon a lease for longer than one year, or for the sale of real property.
- Upon an agreement employing an agent to purchase or sell real property for compensation or a commission.
- Upon an agreement which cannot by its terms be performed within the lifetime of the person making the promise, or an agreement to bequeath property, or to make a will provision.
- Upon a contract or promise to loan money or extend credit, or a contract or promise to change a loan or other extension of credit involving more than $250,000 and not made primarily for personal, family or household purposes.

An action brought on an oral agreement in violation of the Statute of Frauds will be dismissed by the court.

101

Oral Contracts

"An honest man's word is as good as his bond." —Proverb

Contracts may be oral or written. While different rules apply to proving each, one type of contract is not necessarily more enforceable than the other. Under appropriate circumstances, oral contracts are just as enforceable as written contracts.

What is a contract? Simply stated, a contract is an agreement between two or more parties. For a contract to exist, there must be an offer, an acceptance of the offer, and consideration. An offer is a proposal to enter into a contract on the terms contained in the offer. An acceptance is an expression of agreement to the terms of the offer by the person to whom the offer is made. Finally, consideration is a benefit received, or something given up or exchanged, as agreed upon between the parties.

There is no requirement that a contract be in writing to exist. However, certain contracts must be in writing to be enforceable. (Please refer back to Chapter 100 for a list of oral contracts that must be in writing to be enforceable.)

The time period for filing a lawsuit for an oral debt is shorter than the time period for filing a lawsuit for a written debt. In the case of an oral debt, a lawsuit must be filed within three years after the cause of action accrues. The limitation period begins to run at the time the loan is made. In the case of a written debt, the lender has six years after the cause of action accrues to file a lawsuit.

APPENDICES

APPENDIX A
Alcohol Impairment Charts

Alcohol affects people differently. A person's blood alcohol level may be affected by age, gender, physical condition, amount of food consumed and any drugs or medication. In addition, different drinks may contain different amounts of alcohol.

Arizona has set .08% Blood Alcohol Concentration (BAC) as the legal limit for Driving Under the Influence. For commercial drivers, a BAC of .04% can result in a DUI conviction. The following charts should be used as guides to blood alcohol percentages, not as guarantees.

MEN

Approximate Blood Alcohol Percentage

Drinks	Body Weight in Pounds							
	100	120	140	160	180	200	220	240
0	.00	.00	.00	.00	.00	.00	.00	.00
1	.04	.03	.03	.02	.02	.02	.02	.02
2	.08	.06	.05	.05	.04	.04	.03	.03
3	.11	.09	.08	.07	.06	.06	.05	.05
4	.15	.12	.11	.09	.08	.08	.07	.06
5	.19	.16	.13	.12	.11	.09	.09	.08
6	.23	.19	.16	.14	.13	.11	.10	.09
7	.26	.22	.19	.16	.15	.13	.12	.11
8	.30	.25	.21	.19	.17	.15	.14	.13
9	.34	.28	.24	.21	.19	.17	.15	.14
10	.38	.31	.27	.23	.21	.19	.17	.16

Subtract .01% for each 40 minutes of drinking.

One drink is 1.25 oz. of 80 proof liquor, 12 oz. of beer, or 5 oz. of table wine.

WOMEN

Approximate Blood Alcohol Percentage

Drinks	Body Weight in Pounds								
	90	100	120	140	160	180	200	220	240
0	.00	.00	.00	.00	.00	.00	.00	.00	.00
1	.05	.05	.04	.03	.03	.03	.02	.02	.02
2	.10	.09	.08	.07	.06	.05	.05	.04	.04
3	.15	.14	.11	.10	.09	.08	.07	.06	.06
4	.20	.18	.15	.13	11	.10	.09	.08	.08
5	.25	.23	.19	.16	.14	.13	.11	.10	.09
6	.30	.27	.23	.19	.17	.15	.14	.12	.11
7	.35	.32	.27	.23	.20	.18	.16	.14	.13
8	.40	.36	.30	.26	.23	.20	.18	.17	.15
9	.45	.41	.34	.29	.26	.23	.20	.19	.17
10	.51	.45	.38	.32	.28	.25	.23	.21	.19

Subtract .01% for each 40 minutes of drinking.

One drink is 1.25 oz. of 80 proof liquor, 12 oz. of beer,
or 5 oz. of table wine.

Source: National Commission Against Drunk Driving

APPENDIX B
Unified Credit Exemption Amounts

Gift and Estate Tax Table

CREDIT / EXCLUSION FOR ESTATE TAXES		
Year	**Applicable Credit**	**Applicable Exclusion***
2012	$1,772,800	$5,120,000†
2013	$345,800	$1,000,000†

CREDIT / EXCLUSION FOR GIFT TAXES		
2012	$1,772,800	$5,120,000†
2013	$345,800	$1,000,000†

* The exclusion is the amount that can be transferred without tax because of the credit.

† Applicable exclusions pursuant to The Tax Relief, Unemployment Insurance Reauthorization, and Job Creation Act of 2010.

APPENDIX C
Glossary of Civil Lawsuit Terms

Answer A formal written statement filed by the party being sued (defendant) which asserts defenses to the claims made in the complaint. An answer may be accompanied by a counter-claim, which asserts claims by the defendant against the plaintiff.

Arbitration An alternative dispute resolution procedure, involving one or more decision-makers (arbitrators) who decide the claims outside of court. In smaller cases, arbitration is required (referred to as "compulsory arbitration").

Complaint A formal written statement filed by the party who starts the lawsuit (plaintiff) which asserts that party's claims in the action.

Controverting Certificate A document that controverts an opposing party's document. A controverting certificate may be filed in opposition to a plaintiff's certificate regarding compulsory arbitration, or in opposition to a Motion to Set and Certificate of Readiness.

Defendant An individual, partnership, corporation, public entity, public officer, or authorized public agency against whom or which a lawsuit is brought.

Deposition An oral examination of an adverse party or witness under oath, taken by any party prior to trial.

Disclosure Statement A written disclosure of information that each party must furnish to the other within 40 days after the defendant's answer is filed. The disclosure statement must contain specific information concerning the claims and defenses, the identities of witnesses, a description of all exhibits, and other pertinent information detailed in Court Rule 26.1.

Discovery A pretrial procedure used to uncover evidence. Discovery may consist of interrogatories (written questions that must be answered under oath), requests to produce documents or things, requests for admission of facts or law applicable to the case, or depositions.

Interrogatories Written questions that any party may serve upon any other party. The party served is required to respond within 40 days. The response to each interrogatory, unless an objection, must be an answer under oath signed by the person making it.

Judgment A court order that serves as a formal record of the trial court's determination of the case. It fixes the rights and liabilities of the parties to a lawsuit. A judgment is generally entered at the end of a case.

Mediation Another form of alternative dispute resolution, involving a neutral third party (mediator) who listens to the parties and attempts to facilitate a resolution of their disputes. Mediation is not binding unless all the parties agree to the result.

Motion A formal written request asking the court for some form of relief. Motions made during a trial may be oral.

Motion to Set and Certificate of Readiness A court document that requests the assigned judge to set the case for trial and certifies that all discovery has been completed or will be completed in advance of trial. Must be filed to set the case for trial.

Plaintiff An individual, partnership, corporation, public entity, public officer, or authorized public agency that brings a lawsuit.

Pretrial Conference A conference set by the court in advance of the trial. The parties (or their attorneys) usually discuss different aspects of the case with the judge at the pretrial conference.

Subpoena A document issued by the clerk of the court commanding a person to appear for a deposition or trial. Subpoenas may be issued at the request of any party. A subpoena *duces tecum* may also be issued directing a person to produce books, papers, documents, or tangible things specifically designated.

Summons An official court document which requires the defendant to defend against the plaintiff's claims as stated in the complaint. A summons is served upon the defendant with a copy of the complaint.

Endnotes

Part One: Criminal & Traffic Laws; Citizens' Rights and Duties

1. Additional coverages may include uninsured motorist coverage, underinsured motorist coverage, collision coverage, and medical payments coverage. Additional premiums are charged for these optional coverages.

2. An Order of Protection, discussed in Chapter 36, may be obtained to prevent a person from committing an act of domestic violence.

Part Two: Consumer Laws

1. The statutes referenced in this chapter may be obtained from most public libraries in Arizona or from the Arizona State Legislature's Web site, www.azleg.gov.

2. "Ordinary negligence" is based on the fact that one ought to have known the results of his acts, while "gross negligence" rests on the assumption that one knew the results of his acts, but was recklessly or wantonly indifferent to the results.

3. Prior to 1987, a commercial contractor in Arizona was not required to be licensed. Now, however, all contractors must be licensed.

Part Three: Family Law

1. First cousins may marry if both are 65 years of age or older. If one or both first cousins are under the age of 65, they can marry if they

can show proof to a superior court judge that one of them is unable to reproduce.

2. Since the adoption of the Covenant Marriage Act, the author estimates that less than one percent of all marriages in Arizona have been covenant marriages.

3. In addition, the wife's credit probably will be negatively affected by her former husband's failure to pay the debt and resulting collection action.

4. There are about 23,000 divorces and annulments granted each year in the state of Arizona, according to Arizona Department of Health Services records.

5. The court may grant the great-grandparents of the child reasonable visitation rights, too, on finding that they would be entitled to visitation rights if they were the grandparents of the child.

Part Four: Wills and Estates

1. "By representation" means that an heir takes by representation of a deceased parent. For example, three children of a deceased parent would each take by representation one-third of their parent's share.

2. Note: Any designation discussed in this chapter must be made with the financial institution at which the account is located.

3. For a discussion on health care powers of attorney, please see the preceding chapter on health care directives.

Part Five: Civil Lawsuits and Claims

1. Author's Note: Many of the terms used in this chapter are defined in the Glossary of Civil Lawsuit Terms, Appendix C. The reader is encouraged to consult the Glossary as necessary.

2. It should be noted that while most trial work *is* handled by attorneys, individuals may represent themselves in civil actions. Those individuals are subject to the same trial rules as attorneys.

3. A manufacturer or seller of a product may also be liable for negligence. For a discussion on that theory of liability, please refer to Chapter 62.

4. The *common law* is judge-made law, as opposed to *statutory law,* which is legislature-made law.

5. The burden of proof for consumer fraud is *preponderance of the evidence*. This is a lower standard than *clear and convincing evidence*, which is required for common law fraud.

6. Each county has a county recorder. The county recorder is responsible for maintaining all property records within his or her county.

7. A "next friend" or "guardian *ad litem*" is a person who represents the interests of a minor or incompetent person in a lawsuit.

8. The amount in controversy is the amount involved in the case, excluding interest, costs, and awarded attorney's fees.

9. The procedure discussed in this chapter is renewal by affidavit. There is an alternative procedure, renewal by action, but the alternative is seldom, if ever, used.

Part Six: Business Law

1. *Coke* may well be the most famous registered trademark in the world.

2. Some employers do not have to report wages and pay taxes. For example, the members of a limited liability company are exempt, if they have reserved the management of the company to the members. These exceptions are strictly limited, however.

About the Author

Donald Loose is the managing partner of Loose, Brown & Associates, P.C. His law practice is concentrated in the areas of business, litigation and estates, with an emphasis on business-related and construction litigation. He founded Loose, Brown & Associates in 1982. Since then, Don has counseled thousands of individuals and businesses on virtually every area of Arizona law. He is the author of a legal newsletter, and he has taught a college-level business law course. Don has been selected as one of *Arizona's Finest Lawyers*.

Don is a member of the state bars of Arizona and Michigan and is admitted to practice in the courts of those states, as well as the United States Supreme Court. He is a longtime member of the American Bar Association; Maricopa County Bar Association; and the Pima County Bar Association. In addition to his professional memberships, over the years he has belonged to numerous charitable and civic organizations—serving on the boards and as president of two of them.

Don lives with his wife, Nancy, and their twin sons, John and Grant, in Tucson, Arizona. He also maintains a residence in Phoenix, where his firm's principal office is located. You may reach him at don@loosebrown.com, or visit his Web site at www.ArizonaLaws101.com.